The Great Economic Mysteries Book:

A Guide to Teaching Economic Reasoning Grades 9-12

THE EconomicsAmerica AND EconomicsInternational PROGRAMS

CREDITS

Project Director
Mark C. Schug
University of Wisconsin-Milwaukee
Center for Economic Education

Writers
Mark C. Schug
University of Wisconsin-Milwaukee
Center for Economic Education

Richard D. Western
University of Wisconsin-Milwaukee
Department of Curriculum and Instruction

Production
Diana Borders
Desktop Publishing & Design

Reviewers
Bonnie T. Meszaros
University of Delaware
Center for Economic Education and Entrepreneurship

John S. Morton
Arizona Council on Economic Education

Field Test Teachers
Mary Brenzel-Chavez
Milwaukee Education Center
Milwaukee, Wisconsin

Jenny Keats
Roosevelt School
Wauwatosa, Wisconsin

Amy M. Sutliff
Desert Mountain High School
Scottsdale, Arizona

Copyright © 2000, National Council on Economic Education, 1140 Avenue of the Americas, New York, NY 10036. All rights reserved. The activities and worksheets may be duplicated for classroom use, the number not to exceed the number of students in each class. Notice of copyright must appear on all pages. With the exception of activities and visuals, no part of this book may be reproduced in any form or by any means without permission in writing from the publisher. Printed in the United States of America.

ISBN 1-56183-128-X

CONTENTS

Foreword v

Introduction vii

Chapter 1   Economic Reasoning for Kids: An Overview 1

Chapter 2   Using the Mysteries: A Teacher's Guide 7

Chapter 3   Contemporary Economic Mysteries 27

Chapter 4   Public Choice Mysteries 61

Chapter 5   Environmental Mysteries 85

Chapter 6   Writing Your Own Mysteries 103

FOREWORD

Economic reasoning proceeds from basic assumptions about human behavior — made credible by historical evidence — to describe and explain human economic activity. *The Great Economic Mysteries Book: A Guide to Teaching Economic Reasoning Grades 9-12,* is part of a new two-volume set from the National Council on Economic Education (NCEE) which aims to introduce students to the "economic way of thinking" through intriguing mysteries from current events, government, and the environment.

The Great Economic Mysteries Book: A Guide to Teaching Economic Reasoning, Grades 9-12, contains activities that are interactive, reflecting the belief that students learn best through active, highly personalized experiences with economics. Students solve each mystery by using the clues provided and by reference to a logical system of reasoning that applies basic principles of economics. Applications of economic understanding to real-world situations dominate the lessons.

The Great Economic Mysteries Book: A Guide to Teaching Economic Reasoning Grades 9-12, provides teachers with an overview of economic thinking; a model lesson plan for grades 9-12; a guide that states the solution to each mystery; and 35 engaging and often humorous mysteries. Sample mystery titles include "The Case of the Pampered Chickens", "How We Almost Got a Sixth Great Lake", and "Why Air Condition the Air in the Desert?" The mysteries, lessons, and activities are correlated to the *Voluntary National Content Standards in Economics,* which were developed and published by NCEE in 1997.

NCEE is grateful to the authors, Mark C. Schug, Professor of Curriculum and Instruction, and Director of the Center for Economic Education, and Richard D. Western, Associate Professor of Curriculum and Instruction, both at the University of Wisconsin-Milwaukee. NCEE also thanks the Wisconsin Council on Economic Education for its assistance in administering the project.

Since 1949, the National Council on Economic Education, a nonprofit, nonpartisan organization, has been dedicated to increasing the economic literacy of *all* students. This publication builds on five decades of success in delivering economic education in the nation's schools.

Robert F. Duvall, Ph.D.
President and CEO
National Council on Economic Education

INTRODUCTION

This is a book about economic reasoning as it might be taught and practiced in secondary school classrooms. It explains and illustrates a particular approach to reasoning. It shows how students can use this approach to think about problems and to imagine solutions for them. It presents an array of problems, or mysteries, to be used by students in practicing reasoning skills, and it invites teachers and students to supply new mysteries of their own, for extended practice. The field testing we have done to date suggests that many young people especially enjoy moving on to this step—from the given mysteries to ones they've come up with themselves.

Some of the mysteries we present will be familiar to students, reflecting aspects of their experience. Others will challenge students to stretch and think about new things. To help in these efforts, we've built some background information into the problems, in the form of clues or true-false questions. Teachers will decide according to their own circumstances, of course, whether this background information needs to be amplified in particular cases. But we hope nobody will use the mysteries merely as prompts for engaging young people in routine tasks of gathering information. The key to economic reasoning is reasoning, not looking things up.

Reasoning never goes unaccompanied, however. On any occasion that calls for reasoning—in thinking about whether the next pitch will be a curve or a fastball, whether to take the dog for a walk now or after the evening news—all of us try to use what we already know, reasoning from it as a starting point. Experts working in academic and professional fields do the same thing, making deliberate use of their special knowledge. That is why it is never enough to teach students to use generic problem-solving steps. There is no generic procedure for describing problems or brainstorming solutions to them. The describing and brainstorming done in any case will depend, for good or ill, on the outlook and knowledge the problem-solver brings to the task.

Fortunately, in trying to improve our own reasoning skills and in helping children to improve theirs, it isn't necessary to start from scratch. Teachers and children can benefit from the achieved insights of others. If that were not so, nobody could move beyond what Howard Gardner calls the condition of the unschooled mind.

Not surprisingly, the insights featured in *The Great Economics Mysteries Book* are ones formulated originally by economists. We have summarized them in a brief list of principles called the *Handy Dandy Guide*, or sometimes just the *HDG*. These principles represent, in shorthand fashion, the outlook and special knowledge that economists bring to bear on reasoning tasks. In using the *HDG* to describe mysteries and explain them, students begin learning what some people have called the economic way of thinking. It is a way of thinking that can open young people's eyes to new ways of understanding their own world and the public world we expect them, one day, to govern. And, many students say, it is about as much fun as you can have in school.

CHAPTER 1

Economic Reasoning for Kids: An Overview

Is Economics Your Worst Nightmare?

Is the thought of teaching economics your worst nightmare? If it is, you are not alone. Many smart, capable teachers feel the same way. Even those who enjoy teaching government, history, and geography may regard economics as a subject scarier than witches and goblins on Halloween. What might explain this attitude? Is economics inherently remote, dense, and dry?

Not at all. Not necessarily, at least. At key moments in history, economists often have addressed themselves to the analysis of problems that were anything but remote or dry. Adam Smith, the founder of economics, had much to say in 1776 about the most pressing issues of his day—explaining, for example, how trade and the division of labor can increase a nation's prosperity, and arguing that, for Great Britain, the costs of maintaining the American colonies would prove to outweigh the benefits. John Maynard Keynes, seeking to understand and ameliorate the widespread unemployment Great Britain experienced after World War I, argued that deficit spending by governments during periods of recession can foster economic growth and help to bring a nation back to full employment. In subsequent years his theory has been a powerful influence among policy makers in Europe and the United States. During the Great Depression, economists in the United States played an important role in Washington, advising presidents and legislators on policy issues related to labor, agriculture, taxation, corporate monopolies, and welfare. Still more recently, economists have been in the thick of things in the former Soviet Union, advising people there about on-going efforts to modernize the former Soviet-style economies.

But despite this history of engagement with real-world affairs, economics does strike many students today as remote and difficult. In one sense, this is not surprising. After all, economics has been around for a while. It is a mature academic discipline now, one about which economists can speak in detail and at great length—think of all those weighty Econ 101 textbooks! Not only that: as the discipline has matured, economists have sought to be ever more precise in their work, and their search for precision has led them increasingly to the use of rigorous, abstract language, including the language of mathematical operations and models. Macroeconomics, the branch of economics that focuses on whole economic systems, and the branch about which economists tend most to disagree, has become particularly abstract. As a result, even students in Econ 101 now are apt to encounter technical analyses, expressed in compressed, quantitative terms, where they may have expected to find advice about personal finance or general discussions about wealth and poverty.

Where does this leave you? Fortunately, K-12 teachers trying to find their bearings in economics need not choose between the work of Adam Smith and John Maynard Keynes, on the one hand, and the work of technical specialists, on the other. Between the history of economics and its presence in cutting-edge research today, educators can find an impressive set of concepts and principles representing the best insights of the discipline and suitable at the same time for use in curricular planning and day-to-day classroom teaching.

What might these fundamental concepts and principles be? Here are some examples taken from the *Voluntary National Content Standards in Economics* (1997), published by the National Council on Economic Education.

- Productive resources are limited. Therefore, people cannot have all the goods and services they want; as a result, they must choose some things and give up others.

- Effective decision making requires comparing the additional costs of alternatives with the additional benefits. Most choices involve doing a little more or a little less of something; few choices are all-or-nothing decisions.
- Different methods can be used to allocate goods and services. People acting individually or collectively through government must choose which methods to use to allocate different kinds of goods and services.
- People respond predictably to positive and negative incentives.
- Voluntary exchange occurs only when all participating parties expect to gain. This is true for trade among individuals or organizations within a nation, and among individuals or organizations in different nations.

Look back at these five statements and notice what it is that they address: the limits people encounter in striving to satisfy their desires, their need for making choices, the consequences that follow from choosing, the dynamics underlying their transactions with others. Nothing remote or dry in this list of basic human concerns. In the chapters that follow, we'll seek to elaborate that point: economics takes as its subject matter the choices and relationships that matter most to people in their everyday lives.

Right now, however, we want to dwell for a moment on something else you may have noticed about the five statements. The statements have an *edge* to them. Each one *asserts* something: Productive resources *are* limited, voluntary trade occurs *only* when . . ., and so on. The assertions might seem to ring true or false, but they strike few people as bland or inconsequential. They have a probative quality. They cause us to sit up and take notice—to begin thinking about what would follow, in a given case, if one of the statements applied to it.

This assertive, probative quality of our five examples reveals something important about the economic way of thinking. In approaching problems and thinking them through, economists do not start from scratch. They work instead from definite points of departure and they make use of well-established tools in their analyses. They are not only willing but eager, in other words, to work from their disciplinary vantage point.

Doesn't their work violate, then, the norms of objectivity that we associate with honest inquiry and objectivity? Only if you assume that honesty and objectivity depend upon a certain sort of *starting point*—starting with a blank slate or an open mind, setting aside all your assumptions, and so forth. Like most other people who work within academic disciplines, economists do not believe that objectivity in this sense is ever achievable, and they do not seek it. Their norm of objectivity is different. It has to do with facing up to evidence. It is one thing to use established assumptions to get started reasoning out a problem; it is another to check your reasoning against some sort of evidence and to admit that you were wrong if the evidence says you were.

Getting Kids Started

The key assumptions of economics may be stated variously and applied with various emphases, depending on the grade level of the students and other circumstances that bear on teachers' instructional planning. Many curriculum publications of the National Council on Economic Education have used a formulation called the *Handy Dandy Guide for Solving Economic Mysteries* to introduce economic concepts and principles of the sort presented in the *Standards*. The *Handy Dandy Guide* can not do students' thinking for them, but it provides students with a place to begin: a source of hunches to play out against the evidence, and a means of sorting the useful clues out from the useless ones.

Here is one version of the *Handy Dandy Guide*, intended for use with high school students. It is followed by a mystery—the Mystery of the Greedy Teenagers—which we discuss in order to illustrate the uses of the *Handy Dandy Guide* in economic reasoning.

The Handy Dandy Guide
1. People *choose*.
2. People's choices involve *costs*.
3. People respond to *incentives* in predictable ways.
4. People create *economic systems* that influence individual choices and incentives.
5. People gain when they *trade* voluntarily.
6. People's choices have consequences that lie in the *future*.

The Mystery of the Greedy Teenagers

The mystery in this case has to do with teenage babysitters and why parents can't find enough of them:

In the United States there are about 37 million young people between the ages of 10 and 19. People from this age group are the ones most likely to work as babysitters. Yet parents in many neighborhoods today have a hard time finding babysitters. When they are lucky enough to find one, the sitter often charges high prices—sometimes from $6 to $10 an hour. The minimum wage is only $5.15 an hour! Why are today's teenage babysitters so greedy? Who do they think they are?

Is the greed explanation a good one here? Let's work through the *Handy Dandy Guide* and see what light it sheds on this mystery.

1. People *choose*.

This principle may seem merely to state the obvious, but stop and think for a minute about how often you hear people claim that, in one situation or another, they had no choice in the course of action they took. Sometimes the claim about not having a choice helps people to explain their behavior in a manner aimed at avoiding offense or discourtesy. Imagine, for example, that your colleagues have asked you to meet them at a favorite spot after work. You decline, saying that you can't do it tonight; your spouse is expecting you for an early dinner, so you have to get right home. While your response here is courteous and likely to be accepted by your friends, it isn't exactly accurate. You *could* choose not to get home promptly. Under some circumstances—you witness an auto accident, for example, and spend time after the accident providing the police with an account of what you saw—you probably *would* choose not to. But tonight you'd rather get home promptly than spend time hanging out with your colleagues. Stating the point in that way, however, highlights the choice you've made to put your pals in second place. That seems a bit blunt, so you say you *have* to go home; you have *no choice*.

In these matters, young people and adults are much alike. Both are prone to deny that they are making choices in certain cases when that is exactly what they are doing. Both are prone to explain their action in these cases as a matter of necessity—perhaps one imposed by others. Consider, for example, a student who comes late to class and says that he couldn't help it; he missed the bus, or the bus was late, so he had to come late. But the *Handy Dandy Guide* invites us to consider that the student in this case *chooses* to be late. Seem ridiculous? An unfamiliar line of thinking, perhaps, but not ridiculous. The student *could* have done things to get himself to class on time. He could have taken an earlier bus—just in case—or insisted that his parents get up at the crack of dawn to drive him to school early. He *could* have requested permission to sleep over in the classroom!

Not likely, you say. True enough, but likelihood is not the point here. The student did in fact have choices, and the choice he settled for got him to school late. If on-time arrival at school had been much more important to him than it actually was, he would have made the decisions necessary to insure an on-time arrival. How many students would miss a bus if missing it meant staying longer in school or losing an opportunity to meet a favorite athlete or celebrity?

What does this have to do with teenage babysitters? Teenagers who could work as babysitters make choices about whether to accept babysitting jobs or not. Many of them apparently think that the costs of babysitting are not worth the benefits.

2. People's choices involve *costs*.

Decisions come with costs. Always. This is clear enough in the case of decisions to buy something. But the costs that come with decisions aren't always dollar costs. Decide to linger a while at the beach, watching a sunset, and your cost might be, for example, missing a phone call back home. You might count it a good bargain, but that's just another way of saying that missing the phone call was a cost you were willing to pay.

While there are many types of costs, economists stress the importance of opportunity costs. In the case of any decision, the opportunity cost is an individual's second-best choice. It is the road not taken, the alternative not selected. It is not *every* alternative not selected, however. After all, the list of possible alternatives in a given case is endless. The woman who lingered at the beach to watch the sunset could have hurried home to be there for the phone call, or she could have gone off to the library, or she could have gotten the oil changed in her car, or she could have.... Of all these possibilities, her opportunity cost is the most-valued or second best alternative that she didn't select.

When teenagers choose to accept a baby-sitting job, they pay an opportunity cost. That cost is the next-best alternative they give up in order to take the sitter's job. For one teenager, it might be an evening of soccer practice. For another, it might be homework. For another, an evening's work at a higher-paying job. Teenagers who decline to work as sitters apparently aren't willing to pay opportunity costs of this sort.

3. People respond to *incentives* in predictable ways.

Incentives are the key to solving nearly every economic mystery. Economist Steven Landsburg writes in *The Armchair Economist* that "most of economics can be summarized in four words: people respond to incentives. The rest is commentary."

One powerful incentive is money. It is a powerful incentive because it can be exchanged for many other things people desire. It can be used now or saved for future use, spent to paint the town red or invested in a college education, given to charity or saved for retirement. No wonder most people prefer to have more money rather than less. But knowing this about people reveals little to nothing about anybody's character, since people with money may use it wisely or foolishly, on themselves or on others. All we know for sure about the appeal of money, therefore, is that it is widespread.

Not all incentives are monetary, of course. People often perform acts of kindness that involve no material reward. They find satisfaction in knowing they did the right thing. Or people vote on election day or perform volunteer services at a homeless shelter, again for no material reward. They do so, perhaps, to fulfill a sense of duty or obligation. In one sense, however, even behavior of this sort is explained by economic principles; it reflects self-interest, economists say, not selfishness. The self-interest in question is interest in the satisfaction or peace of mind gained through kindness, generosity, and so on.

Do teachers respond to incentives? Many people observe that teachers do their work for relatively low salaries. Therefore, some say, teachers do not respond much to incentives; their motivation is different. Let's examine this argument. A key incentive for teachers is the satisfaction they gain in helping their students learn. These teachers may become irritated when interruptions—school announcements in the middle of class, for example—get in the way of their teaching. Why the anger? Because the interruptions diminish, at least for the moment, the satisfaction that comes with helping students learn.

How do incentives bear on the case of teenagers who choose not to babysit? These teenagers must be responding to incentives other than those attached to babysitting. Young women, for example, now have more opportunities than their mothers had to participate in after-school sports. Young women and young men who want salaried after-school jobs often succeed in finding them. In this climate of expanded opportunities, the cost of babysitting has gone up for teenagers—the opportunity cost, that is. In order to hire babysitters, then, parents must offer pay rates and perks—pizza and videos, perhaps—adequate to compensate teenagers for the opportunity costs created by a host of new incentives.

4. People create *economic systems* that influence individual choices and incentives.

Economic behavior occurs in a climate of rules, formal and informal. The "rules of the game" influence the choices people make in particular cases. Tax laws, for example, influence people's behavior. If a municipal government places a high tax on the width of new buildings, tall and narrow buildings soon begin popping up. If a state government places a large tax on savings accounts, people soon begin keeping less money in their passbook accounts.

How might the "rules of the game" affect teenage babysitting? While many young people do hold jobs, child labor laws restrict their work hours and the types of work they may legally perform. Older teenagers are generally granted more latitude in the job market, and their jobs often pay better than babysitting. This puts pressure on parents to compete for the services of younger teenagers, who may not be permitted to work in retail stores and fast food restaurants.

5. People gain when they *trade* voluntarily.

Economists have discovered that voluntary or free trade creates wealth.

"Voluntary" here refers to a lack of coercion. "Your money or your life!" does not describe an instance of voluntary trade. "Wealth" refers to money, of course, but also to other benefits: When Thelma drives Louise to the airport and borrows Louise's car while Louise is away, both parties may feel better off as a result. Thelma gets the use of a car, and Louise gets her car attended to during her absence. Examples of voluntary trade are everywhere. Purchasing a movie ticket, filling a car with gas, trading paperback books—all involve voluntary trade in which something is exchanged for something else.

The discovery about voluntary trade implies also an opposing proposition that is equally instructive. Involuntary trade decreases wealth, leaving behind only the victors and the vanquished, not a satisfied set of trading partners. Involuntary trade, imposed by one party through the use of force or a threat to use force, differs little from a heist, a theft, a mugging. Slavery in the United States provides a vivid example from our past. Slave traders sold Africans to people who forced them to work, under threat of severe punishment for noncompliance. The harmful legacy of that system, in which the participation of enslaved Africans was obtained only by coercion, is one from which the United States has yet to recover.

What does voluntary trade have to do with babysitting? The couple next-door cannot force teenagers to sit for them. They can only make offers to potential babysitters, in an effort to prompt voluntary trade. Parents who succeed in finding a babysitter will therefore be those offering a sufficient incentive. When this happens, we surmise that both sides gain from the exchange. The parents gain a night together for dinner and a movie. The babysitter gains the promise of payment plus perks—the ubiquitous video and pizza, or perhaps uninterrupted use of the telephone.

Things can go wrong, of course. Because both sides *think* they will gain through voluntary trade does not insure that they *will* gain in fact. The kids could turn out to be terrible brats, so that sitting for them at the agreed-upon rate turns out to be a bad bargain. The sitter could turn out to be irresponsible—spending the evening watching XXX videos, ignoring the kids, and snuffing out cigarettes in the potted plants, so that hiring her or him at the agreed-upon rate turns out to be a bad bargain. In such cases of unsatisfied expectations, the transaction is not likely to be repeated. It would most likely not have occurred in the first place if the participants in question had had the benefit of better information.

6. People's choices have consequences that lie in the *future*.

Despite certain messages conveyed by advertisements and quack therapists, people seldom "live for today." More often, people "live for tomorrow"—or they live, at least, with some thought of tomorrow tucked away in the backs of their minds. We keep our houses painted because the fresh paint looks good, but we know, too, that a coat of paint now may cut down on maintenance costs later. We read a book for pleasure, but we know, too, that we have been hurrying around too much lately, and we might feel better if we set time aside once in a while to sit still and relax.

Teachers routinely report that inservice workshops are notorious for their poor quality. So why do teachers attend them? They are paid to attend them, of course, and future benefits accrue to employees who do what they are paid to do. Also, hope springs eternal: perhaps this *next* inservice will be the one that really does convey useful knowledge. Here, too, the expectation of future benefits provides the criterion for choice.

Similarly, parties to the babysitting transaction are likely to be mindful of decisions and consequences that may follow some time in the future. If parents have found a responsible babysitter at what seems to be a fair price, given the competition, their immediate experience may influence their decisions about whom to call the next time they decide to go out. The immediate experience might alert them also to the possibility that this sitter could be hired for other, more responsible child-care or household jobs in the future. The babysitter may have his or her eye on the future, too. One job now might pave the way for babysitting jobs later with other parents—perhaps even for summer employment—and for good recommendations for other jobs.

The Mystery in Retrospect: What's Greed Got to Do with It?

We have discussed the babysitting example at some length in order to introduce the *Handy Dandy Guide* and to illustrate its uses as a prompt in tasks of economic reasoning. With practice, students can learn to use the *HDG* in ways that lead them to new insights about the curiosities and anomalies in our world that seem to cry out for explanation. The chapters that follow are intended to help teachers provide the necessary practice. Before moving on, however, let us reconsider the mystery with which we began.

Why do parents in many neighborhoods today have a hard time finding babysitters? Are today's teenagers a greedy, money-grubbing lot, compared to their predecessors? Our analysis, aided by the *Handy Dandy Guide*, suggests that teenagers and parents are in a new situation today, and that greed has little to do with the pay and the perks paid to babysitters. Young people today have many possible uses for their time; the decisions they make invariably involve considerations of cost. In order to gain a teenager's voluntary cooperation, parents must provide an attractive incentive: adequate pay and perks. The dollar amounts in question may look high in a given case, but the underlying explanation involves incentives and choices, not greed.

CHAPTER 2

Using the Mysteries: A Teacher's Guide

The Focus on Mysteries

The lessons that follow focus on mysteries—on situations or events in which something seems to be at odds with our sense of what ordinary experience and good judgment would suggest under the circumstances. The students' task is to think the mysteries through and to propose explanations for them. In working at this task, students make use of a set of economic principles—the *Handy Dandy Guide*—and some background information provided by various clues offered in the lessons. The goal is to develop students' capacity for economic reasoning.

In Chapter 1 we introduced the *Handy Dandy Guide* by discussing its relevance to the Mystery of the Greedy Teenagers. Here we'll suggest some general ideas to help you get started working with mysteries of this sort. But first we provide another example of a mystery—one quite different from the babysitting mystery—in order to suggest the wide range of possibilities to which our suggested line of practice may be applied.

The Mystery of the Resourceful Shoppers

In a certain country in the Caribbean, low-income citizens visit upscale restaurants in the evening and order meals for their families. But instead of sitting down in the restaurant to enjoy the meals they have ordered, they package those meals up and take them home. This seems odd. Why would people who don't have a lot of money use restaurants as a source of carry-out food? Wouldn't it be cheaper to buy groceries in bulk and do one's own cooking, at home?

You would think so. Either the restaurant habitues are behaving irrationally, therefore, or their choice in this matter is being influenced by something that isn't immediately obvious. We know that the rules of the game can change the incentives that affect people's choices. Could this idea provide a clue? Suppose that the government in question had decided to subsidize restaurants in order to hold restaurant prices down, thus attracting tourists from the United States and Europe. Suppose further that the same government had pursued economic policies at home that created severe shortages of basic foodstuffs, thus driving grocery prices sky high. Under these circumstances, even low-income people might find it cheaper to buy grilled grouper in a restaurant than to shop for rice and beans at the local market. What seemed odd on the face of it might then come into view as a case of rational choice.

Getting Started

Whether the topic is greedy teenagers or resourceful shoppers, your basic teaching task is to engage students in reasoning about the mystery. In approaching this task you will no doubt devise variations—the possibilities are ample—according to your particular classroom circumstances. Meanwhile, here are some suggestions for getting started.

1. Work with the whole class in introducing the first mystery. Select the mystery carefully for interest value and ease of understanding, so that your students get off to a good start. (The Case of the Pampered Chickens often works well for this purpose.) Use an overhead projector to display the mystery on a screen, if you can, and read the projected mystery aloud, clarifying it as necessary. Then invite the class to speculate on possible explanations. Almost nothing is too outrageous at this point.

2. Display the *Handy Dandy Guide*. (A big wall chart may suit this purpose well, since the *HDG* is something you'll want to refer to frequently. And your students do not need to memorize the points of the *HDG*; chemistry students, after all, do not memorize the periodic table of elements.)

Explain the meaning of each of the principles briefly and walk your students through an application of those principles to the mystery you have selected. (See the Mystery of the Greedy Teenagers in Chapter 1 as an example.) This initial presentation often results in lively discussion.

3. Read the solution to the mystery provided in the *Teachers' Guide* later in this chapter. Then revisit the *Handy Dandy Guide,* highlighting the principles that provide the most help in thinking this mystery through. While all six principles may have a bearing on the mystery, some usually provide more help than others. Encourage your students to develop arguments for the principles they find especially helpful in given cases.

4. When you are satisfied that your students have caught on to the task, introduce a new economic mystery and provide the students with the corresponding Activity sheet. Divide the class into groups and get them working on the new mystery. Remind them to use the *Handy Dandy Guide* and the clues provided. Stress that while all the clues are correct, only a few help to solve the mystery.

5. After an appropriate period for deliberation (brief and sharply focused is better than drawn out and meandering), ask the students in each group to settle on a consensus solution. They should record each solution, along with a brief explanation referenced to the *Handy Dandy Guide* and the clues, on the Activity sheets provided.

6. Reconvene the class as a whole group. Ask a student from each group to report the group's solution to the mystery. Then read the solution provided in the *Teachers' Guide* (see pp. 9-25) and compare it with those proposed by the groups, discussing strengths and weaknesses of each in light of the *Handy Dandy Guide* and the clues.

A Daily Lesson Plan for High School Grades

For accomplishing some tasks, there are fail-safe procedures—algorithms, as mathematicians say. For paginating a manuscript, for example, you could follow an algorithm of this sort: "Put a '1' on the first page, a '2' on the second page, . . ." and so on. *Practicing* such tasks isn't very important; what counts is following the procedure correctly.

The principles of the *Handy Dandy Guide* are not algorithms. They do not provide fail-safe procedures. Instead, they provide speculative instruments, and they can be used well or poorly. *Practice* in using them is therefore very important. In order to gain fluency, flexibility, and boldness in economic reasoning, students need sustained practice in using the *HDG* principles across a wide range of applications.

As a framework for follow-up instruction aimed at providing sustained practice, we suggest the following lesson plan format.

Objectives
1. Students distinguish between relevant and irrelevant clues.
2. Students use relevant clues to help identify the economic principles useful in solving the mystery.
3. Students use principles from the *Handy Dandy Guide* in solving economic mysteries.

Time Estimate
- 30 minutes

Materials
- One transparency of the visual with the mystery.
- For each student, one copy of the Activity sheet which contains the mystery, the clues, and the *Handy Dandy Guide*.
- Provide each student with a copy of the mystery in the Activity. The number of clues varies with each lesson. Assign each student at least one clue. Some teachers clip out the clues and assign one or more clues to each student. While this is more work for the teacher, it tends to add more suspense to the lesson.

Lesson Description
Students describe an economic mystery and discuss various explanations. They use an Activity sheet with a list of clues to help them arrive at a solution for the mystery.

Procedure
1. Explain the purpose of this lesson: students will sharpen their reasoning skills by using economic principles and clues to solve an economic mystery.

2. Remind the group that the task is to use economic reasoning. For example, a key economic principle is that people respond predictably to positive and negative incentives. Economic thinking most often entails discovering the incentives that are influencing people's behavior.

3. Display the Visual to the class. Invite the students to speculate about what the solution to the mystery might be. Briefly review the points of the *Handy Dandy Guide*.

4. Divide the class into small groups. Ask each group to select a discussion leader. Give each group a copy of the corresponding Activity sheet. Then put the groups to work, with these directions:

    A. Their task is to propose a solution to the mystery, explaining their solution by using economic reasoning.

    B. They should first decide which clues provide useful information. Some do and some do not. The students should not get bogged down in arguing over the truthfulness of the clues themselves. Instead, they are only to decide which clues are relevant to solving the mystery.

    C. Each group has a full set of clues. Assign each group member at least one clue. Each group member is responsible for evaluating the relevance of his or her own clue and for leading a discussion within the group of its relationship to the mystery.

5. Monitor the group discussion. You'll probably find that many students will be eager to have their clues matter. Some will go to extremes of tortured logic to argue that their clues are crucial. Remind the students in these cases that this exercise involves sorting out the useful from the irrelevant. Not all information is of equal value.

6. Ask each group to report its solution to the mystery and to justify its choice of the relevant clues. See the *Teachers' Guide* (pages 9-25) for the correct clues.

Closure
Review the main points of the lesson.

Teacher's Guide for Chapter 3
LESSON 1
The Case of the Pampered Chickens

Scientists are constantly looking for ways to improve our lives. They have little time to waste on nonsense. Yet a Texas A&M agricultural engineer has spent some of his time inventing a contact lens for chickens. Other scientists have experimented with playing classical music to barnyard animals.

Are these the stereotypical mad scientists? Why would scientists waste their time with contact lenses for chickens or Mozart for animals when so much really important work needs to be done?

Clues 4 and 8 are important for solving this mystery.

Solution
Economic thinking suggests that there must be rewards for researchers who indulge in such strange behavior. The rules of our economic system are such that individuals who develop new ways to increase productivity may gain rewards for their work (Clue 8). The contact lens research has to do with making egg production more efficient, providing lower costs and higher profits to producers, and lower prices for consumers (Clue 4). Contact lens research is one of several experiments being con-

ducted to find ways to encourage chickens to lay more eggs. When chickens wear these colored contacts, they are calmer and tend to peck each other less; in this more peaceful state of mind, they tend to lay more eggs.

LESSON 2
The Credit Card Mystery
Interest rates change. Yet interest rates on credit card balances remain high relative to other rates, often averaging around 17 percent. Several bills have been introduced in Congress to impose a nationwide ceiling on credit card interest rates.

Why do we have high interest rates on credit cards when other interest rates are so much lower?

Clues 2, 3, 4, and 9 are the most important for solving this mystery.

Solution
Credit cards are convenient for consumers. Credit cards are easy to get. Tests for credit-worthiness are simple to pass. Credit cards are easy to use. These points are related to Clue 4.

Credit card risks are high. Levels of credit card theft and fraud are high (Clue 9). Credit cards are often used to purchase things that are consumed or easily hidden, not to purchase cars or houses that can easily be repossessed (Clues 2 and 3).

Credit card providers understand the risks associated with widely available credit, and they charge higher interest rates as compensation for taking these risks. The higher interest rates act as incentives that encourage providers to continue to offer credit card loans.

Ask your class to predict what would happen if the government imposed limits on the amount of interest these providers could charge. Credit card providers would soon impose higher tests for credit and make credit cards available only to wealthier, low-risk people. In other words, such an action would cause a credit shortage.

LESSON 3
Unsafe at Any Level of Protection
Cars today come loaded with safety equipment: padded dashboards, seat belts, collapsible steering columns, anti-lock brakes, air bags, and so forth.

But recent studies show that antilock braking systems are not reducing the number of accidents people suffer or the costs of those accidents. Similarly, auto crash injuries have increased in number since cars have been equipped with airbags.

Why aren't safer cars producing fewer accidents?

Clue 3 is the most important for solving this mystery.

Solution
Improvements in brakes and other safety features reduce the incentive for safe driving (Clue 3). People are more willing to take risks when they know their cars are safe. Could we change the incentive structure to reward safe driving? Ask your students to explain how driving behavior would change if we were to replace the driver's air bag with a dagger pointed out toward the driver's seat.

LESSON 4
Why Airborne Infants Aren't Required to Buckle Up
Infant airline passengers who ride in their own safety seats fly more safely than those who ride in their parents' laps. Yet the U.S. government does not require the use of safety seats for infants. It has concluded that establishing such a rule would increase the number of infants killed in accidents while traveling.

Why wouldn't requiring safety seats save more babies?

Clues 3 and 4 are most important for solving this mystery.

Solution
Parents respond to incentives when they decide how to travel. If traveling by air meant that parents would have to purchase an extra air ticket for their infant,

they might make other plans—deciding, perhaps, to drive to their destination instead (Clue 3). Even for airborne infants sitting on their parents' laps and not in a safety seat, flying is safer than riding in a car (Clue 4). Thus, the Federal Aviation Administration is saving infant lives by refusing to require the use of safety seats for infants on airplanes. This is a case where doing nothing is the better option when it comes to saving lives.

LESSON 5
Having Many Children or Few

Most people eventually get married and have a family. But sometimes the number of children people decide to have is a puzzle. People in poor nations generally have more children than people in rich nations.

Why do people who can barely pay for life's necessities have more children than people who are more affluent?

Clues 2, 3, 6, and 7 are important for solving this mystery.

Solution
For people in poor nations, the benefits of having children must outweigh the costs. For people in wealthy nations, the costs of having children must outweigh the benefits.

The benefits of having children in a poor nation include the joy children bring to their parents. The children may also be an economic asset, contributing income to the family and looking after their parents in their parents' old age (Clue 3).

The costs of raising children in a poor nation are relatively low. Women in poor nations—owing to relatively low levels of education—often have a low opportunity cost for having children (Clue 2). They give up little in the way of alternative possible uses of their time.

The main benefit of having children in a wealthy nation is the joy the children bring. Children contribute little to family income (Clue 7). The costs of having children include a high opportunity cost for women (many of whom do give up important alternative uses of their time to focus on child care) and high direct costs including the cost of clothing, housing, recreation, and post-secondary education (Clue 6).

LESSON 6
Scarce Health Care in the Inner Cities

At a political rally, Senator Phogbound waxed eloquent about a complicated plan he had introduced to improve health care for low-income residents in America's inner cities and rural areas. The plan would cost billions. As the Senator went on and on, a voice from the audience called out: "Ease up on our immigration restrictions, Senator and more people will have access to health care!" Easing up on immigration restrictions would cost very little.

How could easing immigration rules help to provide health care to those who need it most?

Clues 2, 5, and 6 are the most important for solving this mystery.

Solution
Changing the rules of the game may influence choices and incentives. Many physicians choose not to practice in America's inner cities (Clue 2). If our immigration rules were changed to encourage the immigration of International Medical Graduates (IMGs) to the United States, more health care would be available (Clues 5 and 6). Many newly-arrived physicians would take up neglected family practices, especially in rural areas and in large cities. Moreover, such an increase in physicians would decrease the cost of health care, if nothing else changed.

LESSON 7
Why Boris Couldn't Buy Much with His Rubles

The former Soviet Union was a super power in mineral wealth, military power, and space exploration. Yet this strong and proud nation had difficulty producing simple, commonplace things—good shoes, for example, or good shirts, cars, bread, or French fries.

Why did a super power capable of producing ICBMs

not produce high quality consumer products?

Clues 2, and 8 are the most important for solving this mystery.

Solution
While the former Soviet Union was a super power in mineral wealth, military power, and space exploration, its command economy was driven by decisions made in Moscow. These decisions favored such national goals as keeping a strong military and competing with the West in space exploration. Very little emphasis was placed on producing what consumers wanted (Clue 8). Moreover, the rules of the command system prevented importing goods from the West; as a result, Soviet state enterprises were never exposed to competition (Clue 2).

LESSON 8
Why Would Mexico Want to Trade with the United States and Canada?

The people of Mexico are proud of their heritage, and they dislike outside interference in their affairs. Over the years Mexico has often been in conflict with its prosperous neighbor—the United States. Mexico and the United States have fought a war with each other, have had many border clashes, and have often disagreed about immigration and drug enforcement policies. Moreover, the two nations are economically different. Mexico has a relatively small economy, while the U.S. economy is the world's largest.

Mexico has joined the United States and Canada in agreements aimed at increasing trade among the three countries.

Why would a nation like Mexico, with a proud past and small economy, want to increase trade with the United States—a former enemy with a larger economy?

Clues 4, 5, and 6 the are most important for solving this mystery.

Solution
The North American Free Trade Agreement (NAFTA) significantly reduced trade barriers between voluntary trade among businesses in these nations. The results included more jobs in Mexico and, thanks in part to increased imports from the United States and Canada, lower prices for consumers (Clue 5). The United States also benefited from trade with Mexico; increased exports from the United States produced new jobs (Clue 6).

LESSON 9
The Heart Throb Mystery

Every news stand sells magazines featuring glamorous, stylish people. Many Americans admire these attractive people. Some fantasize about meeting or even dating the heart throbs of *People Magazine*, *Glamour*, *GQ*, and the rest.

Yet social scientists have found that people who are physically very attractive—those who seem most desirable—are less likely to marry than people whose appearance is more ordinary.

You might think the heart throbs would have suitors lined up outside their doors, eager for marriage. Why is this not so? What happens to the heart throbs on the way to the altar?

Clues 2, 3, and 4 are the most important for solving this mystery.

Solution
Though we may not think about it in these terms, dating and marriage have something to do with choices, costs, and attention to future consequences. Highly attractive individuals offer a unique set of costs and incentives to potential suitors. For some suitors, the costs of competing for (and keeping) an attractive spouse are seen as too high (Clues 2 and 4). They prefer to seek a less glamorous spouse. Attractive people themselves face risk in courtship and marriage. They worry that potential suitors are interested only in physical attraction rather than a relationship built on character, respect, and mutual interests (Clue 3). The Heart Throb Mystery is a good one to use around Valentine's Day.

LESSON 10
The Gift-Giving Mystery: Why Not Just Send Money?

You don't have to be Midas or Scrooge to enjoy having money. Money is handy because people can exchange it for other things they want to have. Try getting a rental car or movie tickets on the barter system.

Yet most gift-givers don't give money. Instead they spend time trying to find the right gift, and they often get it wrong.

Why do people struggle to find special gifts for important days like birthdays and holidays when it would be easier and more efficient just to give money?

Clues 3 and 7 are the most important for solving this mystery.

Solution
The incentive to the gift giver is the good feeling that comes with showing affection and making a loved one happy. To many people, money by itself seems to be a less satisfying gift precisely because it is easier to give, requiring little thoughtfulness or care for the special interests of the loved one (Clue 3). That is why money is the preferred gift for strangers—the paper carrier, the waiter or waitress who provides good service—rather than loved ones (Clue 7).

LESSON 11
The Mystery of the Crazy Quilt Air Fares

On a recent flight from Chicago to Tampa, Tim discovered that he had paid twice as much for his ticket as the woman seated beside him. Tim checked further, asking five other passengers about their tickets, and he found that each of the five had paid a different price. One person was flying "free" with frequent flier miles.

What is going on here? Why do different passengers pay different prices for exactly the same flight?

Clue 2 is the most important for solving this mystery.

Solution
Airlines do charge different prices to different people for the same product. Actually, many firms do. Some grocery stores offer lower prices to coupon clippers, for example, and some fast food restaurants, hotels, and ski resorts offer discounts to senior citizens.

Why do airlines charge different prices for the same flight? The different fares are largely a reflection of the incentives facing the traveler and the airline. Some customers book airfares well in advance. They shop around. They travel at off-peak times. They are willing to accept connections others might reject. As a result, these travelers get lower fares, and the airlines gain the security of knowing some flights are at least partially sold out.

Other customers are more constrained. An unexpected crisis, for example, may cause a business person to book a last-minute flight. The benefit of getting from Chicago to Tampa is so large to our business traveler that he or she believes the high price tag is well worth it.

LESSON 12
Why the Kid Who Skipped College Earns Big Bucks Playing Games

Many professional athletes never finish college. Some go directly into professional sports from high school. Yet professional athletes are frequently paid millions of dollars. Annual salaries for professional football players range from a few hundred thousand to several million dollars. The story is much the same among professional athletes in basketball and baseball.

Yet other people who perform worthy service—nurses, police officers, firefighters, and teachers—receive incomes far short of the amounts paid to professional athletes.

What is wrong with our values? Why are grown men and women paid millions of dollars to play kid games?

Clues 2 and 5 are the most important for solving this mystery.

Solution
Many people obviously derive pleasure from watching professional athletes perform. Sports fans pay a lot in ticket prices; some also purchase special TV sets for home viewing (Clue 5). While people in other walks of life perform all sorts of worthwhile services, few people would pay much to watch them at work. Moreover, the skills possessed by a top professional athlete are rare (Clue 2). While many of us perform admirably as nurses, teachers, stock brokers, and so on, few can hit curve balls out of the park or make backhand passing shots that tick the baseline, consistently. These forces—consumer demand for watching great athletes, and the limited supply of top athletic talent—help to explain the high pay some athletes earn.

LESSON 13
What's in a Name?
Many consumers love to buy brand name products. They enjoy the quality of the products at the price they pay.

But wait a minute. Why buy Hallmark Cards, Ivory Soap, Coca Cola, or Wheaties? Consumer advocates tell us that many non-brand name products—such as store brands—are nearly identical to their brand name rivals and almost always cost much less.

Why don't cost-conscious consumers ignore all the brand name hype and save money by buying the store brand?

Clues 4 and 5 are the most important for solving this mystery.

Solution
Comparison shopping—studying how products compare on price and quality without regard for brand names and advertising—is certainly a sensible thing for shoppers to do. However, it does entail a cost—the cost of obtaining the information in question (Clue 4). Some consumers are willing to pay more to be sure they are getting the product they expect. For whatever reason, they choose not to experiment with new products or compare one to another. They do not believe that the cost of gaining additional product information (which may or may not help them make a more satisfactory purchase) is worth the benefit others associate with comparison shopping.

Producers of brand name products are very aware of the decisions being made by their loyal customers. Brand name producers try to satisfy their customers' expectations regarding consistent quality at the expected price (Clue 5). They often face stiff competition, so it is in their interest to invest heavily in maintaining the quality and consistency their customers expect.

LESSON 14
Why Don't All Students Study Hard at School?
Most people know that higher levels of formal education go along, on average, with higher incomes for both men and women. People who complete high school, for example, earn more income than people who do not. People who complete a year or two of college earn more than those who do not. People who complete a college degree earn more than those who do not.

Yet many high school students seem to care very little about their education. Many choose not to study very hard. Some even drop out of school.

Since the link between education and income is well established, why do some high school students disdain education?

Clues 6 and 8 are the most important for solving this mystery.

Solution
Many American students choose not to study very hard. They have decided that for them the benefits are not worth the costs. What are the costs of not doing very well in high school? In some respects,

the costs are not all that great. Many students with mediocre high school grades still find their way into college (Clue 6). And employers rarely pay attention to high school transcripts (Clue 8). When faced with the choice of whether to study hard or not, many students decide it is not worth it.

In some states people are experimenting with ways to rearrange the incentive structure. How might this work? Imagine that a student could not be admitted to any form of state-funded post-secondary education unless he or she attained certain minimum scores on external examinations. Imagine further that the state's most coveted post-secondary programs of study were available only to students with top examination scores. Would changes of this sort affect students' decisions about whether or not they should work hard in high school?

LESSON 15
Why Are ATMs Everywhere?

Automated teller machines (ATMs) are nearly everywhere. It is hard to pump gas or visit a convenience store and not be reminded of how easy it is to get cash or make a bank transaction.

Even people living in rural areas, places where ATMs were not to be found until the 1990s, now have easy access to cash and other services through the ubiquitous ATMs.

Where did all the ATMs come from? How is it that, almost overnight, ATMs have popped up everywhere—even in small towns like Townsend, Wisconsin, population 500?

Clues 1, 3, 6, and 8 are the most important for solving this mystery.

Solution

ATMs were relatively rare in the early 1990s. This is not a surprise when you consider that the expense of operating ATMs exceeded the income they produced at that time (Clue 8). Charging fees to non-customers provided an incentive for ATM owners to offer more services (Clue 3). ATM owners quickly learned that far fewer transactions would be necessary in order to make a profit if they charged fees to non-customers (Clue 6). The charging of fees, an idea much disliked by some, provided sufficient incentive to encourage ATM owners to expand their services to small towns across the nation.

Ask your class to predict what would happen if the government did abolish ATM fees. (ATM providers in that case would have less incentive to offer their service. They would provide fewer ATMs and cut back on ATM maintenance. Fees for other bank services would probably increase.)

LESSON 16
Why Everything but the Kitchen Sink Gets Stashed in the Overhead Luggage Bins on Airplanes

Airlines periodically clamp down on people who try to pass off small pianos or lawn mowers as carry-on luggage. It is easy to understand why the airlines get worried. Some passengers try to carry everything from banjos to lobster crates on board their flights. The heavy, awkward bags they stuff into the overhead luggage bins can be downright dangerous as they shift around during the flight or fall down on unsuspecting passengers when the compartment doors are opened.

But perhaps the passengers are not to blame. After all, if they check their luggage they incur a risk of losing it or having to wait a long time for it to show up at the luggage carousel. They also incur a risk of breakage or theft of valuable items.

To date, the solution proposed by the airlines is to do a better job of enforcing their rules about size-limits for carry-on bags.

In an industry sophisticated enough to deal with astrophysics, the coordination of schedules across multiple time zones, the vagaries of complex weather systems, and the mysteries of the microwaved omelette, is there really no good way to solve the on-board luggage problem? Can you use economic thinking to do better?

Clue 5 is the most important for solving this mystery.

Solution

The problem with overhead compartment space on airlines is that no one has a firm, established right to use them. That is why the scramble for the overhead bins is a free-for-all. The overhead luggage bins are what economists call a commons. No one has enforceable rights to use any given space in the bins. As is the case with other commons areas—think of over-grazing on government-owned pasture land or the over-fishing of fisheries—passengers have an incentive to overuse the overhead bins.

What is the solution from an economic perspective? Allow passengers to purchase the right to use space in the overhead compartments. This procedure would provide the necessary incentives to solve many problems that plague air travelers now. If passengers had to pay for their use of the overhead bins, they would tend to economize. More passengers would check their bags voluntarily. Those choosing to "rent" luggage space in the overhead bins could count on finding it; they would not need to charge rudely down an aisle, racing to claim a vacant space ahead of the guy with the tuba or the stuffed moose head. Flight attendants would be relieved of the disagreeable task of playing luggage cop among aggressive, uncooperative passengers.

The change would be good for the airlines. Somebody would need to perfect a method for selling and monitoring space-use under the new system, but the innovative airlines would gain a competitive edge and a new source of revenue in their very competitive industry.

Teachers' Guide for Chapter 4
LESSON 1
The Electoral College Mystery

In the American system of government, majority rule is a fundamental principle of democracy. Yet in presidential elections we continue to use the Electoral College—an undemocratic institution. Under some circumstances, Electoral College procedures permit the election of a candidate who has not earned a majority of the national popular vote.

Why does the world's greatest democracy tolerate such an undemocratic institution?

Clues 1, 4, 6, and 8 are the most important for solving this mystery.

Solution

Politicians ordinarily want to be re-elected. Their wish to be re-elected creates a strong incentive for them to keep the voters back home happy. For members of Congress who represent states with relatively small populations (e.g., Alaska, Delaware, Hawaii, Maine, New Hampshire, Montana, Nevada, New Mexico), one way to keep the voters at home happy is to preserve the Electoral College, since the Electoral College guarantees that even the least populous state will have some clout (no fewer than three electoral votes) in presidential elections (Clue 8).

But why don't members of Congress from large-population states do away with the Electoral College by proposing the necessary action and then outvoting the others? It would take a constitutional amendment to get rid of the Electoral College (Clue 1), and passing a constitutional amendment would require support from the members of Congress representing small-population states (Clue 8). Besides, large-population states also benefit from the Electoral College, since presidential candidates make special efforts to win in the large states (e.g., California, New York, Pennsylvania, Texas) and thus capture the many electoral votes those states control.

Even presidents are apt to see something good in the Electoral College. For newly-elected presidents, the winner-take-all nature of the Electoral College state-by-state elections (Clue 4) may convey a stronger impression of a voter mandate (Clue 6) than the impression conveyed by the total popular vote.

LESSON 2
Where Did the Mortgages Go?
In the 1970s, a law in the state of Illinois prohibited lenders from charging more than 8 percent interest on home mortgages. The purpose of this law was to make home-buying more affordable for people earning low incomes. However, by the mid-1970s, people wanting to buy homes in Illinois found it almost impossible to get home loans from state bankers.

This seems odd. People who lend money can't make any money themselves unless they issue loans.

What happened to the mortgages in Illinois? Why did people in the money lending business not want to issue loans?

Clues 1, 2, 4, and 7 are the most important for solving this mystery.

Solution
Bankers have many choices about how to use bank deposits. One choice is to use deposits for mortgage loans to bank customers. Interest rates can act as incentives (encouraging this choice) or as disincentives (discouraging it) (Clue 2). It depends on the interest rates banks are permitted to charge for the loans they issue (Clue 4). In the 1970s, some interest rates rose above levels set by law (Clue 7). If bankers are not permitted to set interest rates for home mortgages at market levels, they will look elsewhere for better uses of deposit funds (Clue 1). They might invest in real estate, offer mortgage loans to people in other states, purchase securities, issue loans for automobile purchases, and so on.

LESSON 3
The Mystery of the Politicians Who Can't Say No
During the 1980s, the U.S. federal government approved spending levels that created huge federal budget deficits. Most economists agree that these large deficits caused many economic problems, pushing inflation and interest rates up.

Why would government leaders approve levels of spending that they know hurt the economy?

Clues 1, 2, 4, and 9 are the most important for solving this mystery.

Solution
The rules of the game provide incentives that influence politicians in their decisions about spending programs. Politicians compete to gain campaign contributions and to get the votes they need to win elections (Clue 4). Their incentive is to get elected and stay in office (Clue 1). Interest groups compete for influence among politicians and other officials. Their incentive is to shape policy according to their interests (Clue 9). In this context, individual voters have less incentive than politicians and interest groups have to pay attention to spending proposals.

Suppose, for example, that a voter hears or reads about a proposed increase in federal funding for road construction, and suppose further that the project in question looks unnecessary or unwise to the voter. He or she still is not likely to spend much time opposing it, since the trade-off in costs and benefits would not be favorable. The cost of engaging in opposition might be considerable (attending meetings, writing letters, making telephone calls), whereas the benefits associated with defeating the project might amount to very little in tax-savings per individual taxpayer. In contrast, however, the benefits of the project might be huge for construction-related industries and workers, and they might be willing to throw their support behind any politician who supports the project (Clue 2).

LESSON 4
Is Parking Really Free in Fargo?
In a gesture aimed at banishing an annoyance familiar to people who live in big cities, North Dakota legislators voted in 1999 to retain the state's ban on parking meters. One state Senator said that local government shouldn't be able to collect money for parking on public streets. Like driving on public roads, parking on public streets should be free. This sounds too good to be true. Why don't cities

and states everywhere guarantee free parking?

Maybe it is too good to be true. Is parking really free in Fargo?

Clues 1 and 8 are the most important for solving this mystery.

Solution
The curbside space along city streets has, potentially, many uses (Clue 1). It could be used to add another lane to the street, perhaps a bicycle lane. It could be sold or leased to shop owners who wish to expand their operations. Using the space for one of these purposes means not using it for the others (Clue 8). The unselected use is the opportunity cost of the choice that is made. Since an opportunity cost of this sort is inevitable, parking is not free in Fargo, even if city officials say that it is.

LESSON 5
The Mystery of the Missing Pubs
Pubs are central to social life in Ireland. They serve as social centers for neighborhoods, providing people with places to meet for business and pleasure.

Ireland in the 1990s has had a strong economy. The "Celtic Tiger" is the envy of Europe. Given the attachment of many Irish people to the pubs, and given the recent strength of Ireland's economy, you might suppose you could find a pub on every corner in Irish towns and cities. But generally this is not so. Even in Dublin, there are some neighborhoods with only a handful of pubs to serve thousands of people.

Why are there so few pubs in Dublin?

Clues 4, 7, 8, and 9 are the most important for solving this mystery.

Solution
Pub owners in Ireland compete with one another to sell food and beverages to their customers. The more pubs, the more competition. But competition is reduced by laws aimed at reducing drinking (Clue 4). In keeping the number of pubs down, these well-intentioned laws protect established pub owners from widespread competition (Clues 7 and 8). Pub owners thus have an incentive to keep the restrictions in place, since they benefit from the protection it affords them (Clue 9).

LESSON 6
How We Almost Got a Sixth Great Lake
Every school student knows there are five Great Lakes. They remember the lakes easily by recalling "HOMES," the letters of which stand for Lake *H*uron, Lake *O*ntario, Lake *M*ichigan, Lake *E*rie, and Lake *S*uperior. This is common knowledge. Yet, Mr. Patrick Leahy, a United States Senator from Vermont, believes that Lake Champlain, which borders Vermont, New York, and Canada, is also a Great Lake. "Vermonters have always considered Lake Champlain the sixth Great Lake," he declared in 1998. Then he undertook an effort to have Lake Champlain officially designated as a Great Lake.

Why would a U.S. Senator think there are six Great Lakes when school children know that is not true?

Clues 6 and 9 are the most important for solving this mystery.

Solution
In order to gain re-election, men and women elected to serve in Congress seek votes from people in their home states. Their interest in re-election creates a strong incentive to support federal funding for projects in their home states and districts. In 1998, Senator Patrick Leahy discovered what looked like a new way to pursue federal research dollars for Vermont. He tried to have Lake Champlain, which borders Vermont, officially redefined as one of the Great Lakes (Clue 9). If Lake Champlain had been so designated, the change would have allowed researchers in Vermont to compete for research funds made available by the National Sea Grant Program (Clue 6).

LESSON 7
The Mystery of the Voters Who Don't Vote
Americans are known around the world for their love of liberty and democracy. Many Americans

have fought and died to protect their system of government and way of life. Free elections are central to that system of government. Together with safeguards for protecting individual rights, free elections are the heart of American democracy.

Yet many Americans do not vote. Only about half of all eligible voters vote in presidential elections, for example.

Why don't more Americans vote?

Clues 2, 3, and 4 are the most important for solving this mystery.

Solution
People decide whether to vote or not vote, taking into account the costs and benefits associated with the choice. What does it cost to vote? Some time and effort spent registering, gathering information about the candidates (Clues 2 and 4), waiting in line at the polling station (Clue 3), and so forth. Not a high cost, you might say, especially not for citizens who value their participation in the electoral process. But many citizens see little benefit in such participation. The odds are that no single vote will determine the outcome of an election, they say (Clue 6), and the outcomes don't matter all that much to them anyway. Any cost at all, then, seems too much. Let others do the voting, these non-voters say, in effect; we'll "free ride" on the good citizenship of the voters and benefit as much or as little as they do from the outcomes.

Just for fun, you might invite your class to discuss possible ways of reducing the cost of voting. For example: what might the effect be of holding major elections on national holidays? Would a scheduling change of this sort increase or decrease the cost to voters?

LESSON 8
The Corny Fuel Mystery
In the midst of the energy crisis of the late 1970s, the U.S. federal government hit on a new idea. Researchers had found ways to mix ethanol—a fuel distilled from corn—with gasoline. This discovery raised hopes that this new fuel mixture would reduce the amount of gasoline Americans used, thus decreasing United States demand for foreign oil while improving air quality. To encourage the use of ethanol, the federal government provided a subsidy to fuel producers by reducing the gasoline tax on fuel made with the ethanol mixture.

A study done in 1997 by the General Accounting Office (GOA) of the federal government showed that the ethanol subsidy was expensive (it had cost taxpayers $7 billion since 1979) and did little to improve the environment or reduce imports of foreign oil. However, efforts to abandon the ethanol subsidy have failed to gain approval in Congress.

Why would the United States government provide subsidies for the production of an alternative fuel that does not help the environment, does not reduce consumption of foreign oil, and costs taxpayers billions of dollars?

Clues 2, 3, 4, 5, 6, and 9 are the most important for solving this mystery.

Solution
A government subsidy creates a strong incentive among those positioned to claim it (Clues 4, 5, and 9). While the ethanol subsidy seems large, few taxpayers are likely to notice its effect, since the cost of the subsidy is spread out over many people. On the other hand, the producers of ethanol are very aware of the benefits in jobs and income that the subsidy confers on them. Given any threat to those benefits, they get busy alerting politicians to their interest in the matter (Clue 6). Elected officials from the Midwest find it difficult to resist pressure arising from interest groups back home (Clues 2 and 3).

LESSON 9
The Urban Housing Mystery
While most American cities provide an adequate range of housing possibilities for their citizens, some do not. In New York City, people looking for a place to live typically have a hard time finding apartments. Some

of the apartments they find are ones you wouldn't want—units without sinks or hot water, for example. The problem is not a lack of space. New York City has block after block of abandoned apartment buildings.

At the same time, some New Yorkers live in luxury apartments and pay low rents. For example, a 1993 news report stated that former New York City Mayor Ed Koch paid $441 per month for an apartment worth about $1,200 per month at market rental rates.

Why do some New Yorkers face a housing crisis while others are secure in choice apartments, paying low monthly rent?

Clues 1, 2, 6, 7, and 8 are the most important for solving this mystery.

Solution
Building apartments and renting them out to tenants involves making choices. The money put into apartments could be put somewhere else. Rent controls affect the decisions people make in these cases (Clues 1 and 2). A ceiling on rental rates creates a disincentive, discouraging some people from entering or staying in the rental properties business. As a result, some existing apartments will be abandoned or allowed to fall into disrepair, and fewer new apartments will be built (Clue 6). At the same time, rents for non-rent-controlled apartments will be bid up, owing to the shortage created by the rent controls. So why doesn't the City of New York abandon rent controls? Tenants who live in rent-controlled apartments benefit greatly from paying below-market rates (Clues 7 and 8). They support rent controls, and they put pressure on government officials to keep the current system in place.

LESSON 10
The Mystery of the Unwanted Melons
In the early 1990s, some U.S. farmers who ordinarily grew cotton and peanuts began planting crops that were unusual for them—squash and melons, for example. Many of these farmers did not take good care of their new crops. They planted them at odd times, did not irrigate them, and generally did not attend to them. In fact, they hoped they would never harvest these new crops.

Why would farmers plant crops they do not want to harvest?

Clues 2, 3, and 10 are the most important for solving this mystery.

Solution
The government program that compensates farmers for crop failures creates an incentive (Clues 2 and 3), encouraging some farmers to plant crops that they hope will fail (Clue 10).

LESSON 11
Why Can't You Buy A Car on Sunday?
Shopping during weekdays is difficult for today's double-income families. Yet the law in 21 states requires car dealerships to remain closed on Sundays. This may seem odd. Most often business leaders claim they do not want government to interfere with their business practices. Yet when one Minnesota legislator proposed that car sales be permitted (not required) on Sundays, he drew strong opposition from the Minnesota Auto Dealers Association.

Why would people who sell cars not want to sell them on Sunday?

Clues 3, 4, 5, and 9 are the most important for solving this mystery.

Solution
Information isn't free. It costs something to collect information—your time, if nothing else (Clues 3 and 5). By keeping closed on Sundays, car dealerships narrow the window of time within which potential buyers may gather information about the price of a car and its other features. You can walk around a dealer's lot on a Sunday afternoon and kick tires and examine sticker prices, of course, but sticker prices reveal little about actual sale prices or the complicated details of leasing arrangements (Clue 4). To check such details out, and to do comparison shopping, potential customers have to shop during the week or on Saturdays—times when they most likely have many other things they'd like to

do. Keeping closed on Sundays, in other words, increases the cost to the potential buyer who wants to collect information. He or she must take time off from work or give up time on Saturday in order to visit car dealerships when they are open. Some buyers are not willing to pay this cost. Car dealerships benefit accordingly, since buyers who operate on the basis of limited information are apt to pay more for the cars they buy or lease. Keeping closed on Sundays helps the dealerships in maintaining this edge (Clue 9).

Teachers' Guide for Chapter 5
LESSON 1
Why Haven't We Run Out of Natural Resources?

The earth today supports about 6 billion people. Most of these people live in a condition of poverty, lacking adequate food, water, housing, and medical care. As this population grows and its needs increase, many people fear that increasing demand for the earth's resources will deplete those resources drastically. Some scientists in the 1970s predicted, for example, that the world would run out of oil and many important minerals by the 1990s.

After the close of the 1990s, however, things look different. There is little talk today about exhausting our mineral supplies. Prices for most commodities have been stable, suggesting a stable supply. Oil reserves have actually increased. People in impoverished places continue to face shortages, but those shortages have nothing to do with natural resources. Every recent famine, for example, has been caused by civil war, ethnic disputes, or natural catastrophes—not the exhaustion of natural resources.

How can this be? If our natural resources are finite and the world's population is growing, why haven't we run out of natural resources?

Clues 4, 5, and 8 are the most important for solving this mystery.

Solution
Prices act as incentives, influencing people's decisions. When prices for natural resources go up, consumers face an incentive to cut back on their use of those resources—as they did in the 1970s when the price of oil increased (Clue 4). At the same time, rising prices create an incentive for producers. It is an incentive to earn profits by increasing production through the use of improved technology to find new reserves (Clue 5). These price-related incentives are powerful. Profits provide natural resource producers with an incentive to develop new technologies that reduce the costs of production and keep prices low (Clue 8).

LESSON 2
Why Air Condition the Air in the Desert?

Water is a scarce resource. It is precious, especially in arid places and in areas where many people live. Yet in upscale shopping centers and resort areas in the southwestern United States, people try to cool the hot summer temperatures by using misters to emit a light spray of water into the air above sidewalks and patios, thus taking the edge off the desert heat.

Why would people in the middle of the desert use their scarce water resources to "air condition" the outdoors?

Clue 1 is the most important for solving this mystery.

Solution
In using natural resources, people are influenced by price. Higher prices create an incentive to conserve resources; lower prices create an incentive to use them. Water in the desert really is a scarce resource, but it doesn't *seem* scarce because its price is relatively low. People use it extravagantly, therefore, almost as if it were free. This illusion of free or low-cost water is created by government policies that keep the price of water artificially low. If prices for water in the desert were determined by market forces, those prices would go up, and the incentives in question would change. Water users would be encouraged to use water more frugally, and suppliers of water would be encouraged to find new ways of increasing the supply. In this respect,

21

water is like oil. Oil prices in the United States are determined by market forces, and the buying and selling of oil is commonplace. As a result, the oil crisis of the 1970s is now a faded memory, and people who use oil products pay for what they use.

LESSON 3
Why Grow Rice in the Desert?
We think of farmers as sensible, practical people, inclined to make prudent decisions about their work. But farmers sometimes make decisions that seem very strange. For example, farmers in California grow large crops of rice (which requires a great deal of water) in the desert (the Sacramento Valley).

Why would farmers grow rice in the desert?

Clues 1, 2, and 3 are the most important to solving this mystery.

Solution
On the face of it, nothing could be more odd than farmers choosing to grow rice in a desert, unless perhaps it were vintners choosing to grow cabernet sauvignon grapes in the Jack Pine forests of northern Minnesota. But unusual incentives are at work here, and in light of those incentives the rice paddies in the desert do not look so odd after all. Rice farmers have negotiated an agreement with the U.S government that permits them to purchase water at a very low price (Clues 2 and 3). Thus, even though water in the desert is scarce, these farmers obtain it at a low cost. The low costs mean that rice grown in the desert can be a highly profitable crop (Clue 1) despite the arid environment in which it is grown. The problem in this mystery is much like the one described in Lesson 2. In each case, artificially low prices for water encourage extravagant uses of water. In each case, market prices for water would create an incentive for more frugal uses of water. In each case, people who benefit from their access to cheap water maintain their advantage through political activity. And in each case the costs of providing cheap water are spread out over such a large population of taxpayers that the cost per taxpayer will scarcely be noticed. The pattern of large, concerted benefits for an influential few, along with small, diffuse costs paid by many taxpayers, means that rice paddies and mist sprays are unlikely to disappear from the deserts any time soon.

LESSON 4
The Tragedy of the Commons
Wildlife are in danger in many parts of the world.

* Fishing fleets catch so many wild salmon that the species is threatened.
* In some parts of Africa, elephants and other animals are hunted by poachers, despite government bans on hunting.
* The world's population of whales is in danger

Why are so many wild animals endangered?

Clues 3 and 4 are the most important for solving this mystery.

Note to the Teacher
Before you discuss solutions to this mystery, consider spending a few minutes explaining the mystery's title, "The Tragedy of the Commons." It is an expression hearkening back more than 150 years to a time when William Frank Lloyd, a political economist at Oxford University, commented on the devastation of common grazing pastures in England. "Why," he asked, "are the cattle on a common so puny and stunted? Why is the common itself so bare-wore, and cropped so differently from the adjoining enclosures?" The reason was that farmers using common pastures tended to *overuse* them—grazing too many cattle on them—because it cost the farmers little to do so. The lack of individual ownership of grazing pastures created the incentive for overuse. In 1968, Garrett Hardin reflected on the problem Lloyd had identified. Hardin described it as the tragedy of the commons. Since then, the term has come into general use among economists. In this lesson we invite you to consider its applicability to problems involving species preservation.

Solution
From an economic perspective, the problem presented by each case in Lesson 4 is one of insuffi-

cient or perverse incentives. The incentives in play do not encourage people to protect the environment (Clue 3). Indeed, in each case, some incentives encourage people to overuse or abuse the threatened resource—salmon, elephants, and whales.

The incentives would change for the better if a way could be found to establish private ownership rights or something close to private ownership rights (Clue 4) for threatened resources. When nobody owns a population of fish, for example, it is in the interest of a fisherman to catch as many fish as possible. Not to do so is to leave fish for others to catch. In other words, fish owned by nobody—like wild salmon off the American Northwest coast—have no protectors. If ownership rights could be established, the owners of the fish could use the legal system—courts and appropriate law enforcement officers—to protect their valuable property.

But who would protect the fish from their owners? Couldn't people who owned fish simply harvest every one of them? Couldn't they take the money and run? If they did, they would destroy their own property, depriving themselves of any future use of it. The prospect of future use—to continue fishing or to resell the ownership rights to the fish—would create an incentive to protect the fish. In this respect, fishermen would resemble farmers. Farmers are not known for their tendency to wipe out their cows and chickens or to destroy their wheat fields.

Some experiments with ownership rights for fishermen have been initiated in New Zealand and in the Great Lakes area of the United States. In these experiments, a system of quotas and licenses is established, offering fishermen something like a property right in local fisheries. The participating fishermen pay for a license which allows them to catch a quota of fish legally. If there are too many fishermen working a given fishery, the fees from license sales are used to buy out some fishermen until the number is reduced sufficiently to allow the fishery to recover.

In other parts of the world, similar systems provide local people with ownership rights to wildlife. African villagers holding ownership rights to an elephant population, for example, may harvest animals legally and may sell hunting permits to others. In such a system, the incentives encourage protection of the elephants. Since the villagers' future benefits depend upon the elephants, the villagers begin to act as prudent owners—refusing to cooperate with poachers and cooperating with legal authorities to protect their valuable property.

Could ownership rights be used to protect whale pods from illegal hunting? Given the expanse and the depths of the world's oceans, it is obviously an idea marked by challenging problems. But cattle once ranged widely over vast expanses of land in the American West, and ownership rights for the cattle were established by a legal system that involved cattle branding. It is possible, similarly, to imagine an ownership system involving electronic ownership tags placed on whale pods, along with an international system for trading ownership rights. In this way, once again, the incentives would favor the whales, since whale owners would have an interest in protecting their valuable property. Environmental groups also could purchase whale pods in such a system, in order to protect their whales against all harvesting; this tactic is already in use by nature conservancy groups who purchase land in order to protect it from development.

LESSON 5
The Dark Side of Curbside Recycling

Many Americans are taught at an early age about the importance of recycling. Most of us dutifully separate paper, plastic, glass, and cans and haul these things down to the curb on the assigned day of the week. We all feel better knowing we are helping our community and the environment.

Yet some critics have argued that curbside recycling may actually harm our community and the environment.

How could there be a downside to something as benign as recycling? How can recycling harm our environment?

Clues 2, 3, and 4 are most important for solving this mystery.

Solution
Curbside recycling programs involve a change in the rules governing disposal of solid waste. While the programs have generally been popular, they also have given rise to some unexpected problems. For example, since there is no market for some of the materials collected in recycling programs, local governments often fail to recover the costs they incur in picking these materials up and storing or disposing of them (Clue 2). Moreover, it is not clear that the gains in environmental quality produced by curbside recycling are greater than the environmental costs (in energy use, for example) generated by recycling programs (Clue 4). Finally, in some communities, curbside recycling has destroyed one way in which community groups have traditionally raised revenue for their various projects (Clue 3).

As we continue to gain experience with curbside recycling programs, the ongoing question will be whether the benefits they produce are worth the costs they generate.

LESSON 6
The Bright Side of Urban Sprawl
Americans continue to be mobile people, relocating themselves to outlying areas beyond the established suburbs. Yet it is fashionable in some circles to hate urban sprawl. The very term—"urban sprawl"—sounds bad. To many Americans it conjures up images of endless strip malls and congested roadways, crowding out a dwindling supply of open spaces. Some politicians have argued for an end to unregulated urban sprawl, proposing instead that growth should conform to plans for "smart growth."

If urban sprawl is such a bad thing, why do so many Americans choose to be a part of it?

Clues 1, 3, and 8 are the most important for solving this mystery.

Solution
People looking for a place to live have an obvious interest in affordable housing. The prospect of affordable housing in outlying areas creates an important incentive that encourages people to "leap frog" to new suburbs (Clue 1). People who make the leap do so because they determine that the housing benefit they gain outweighs the costs involved, for example, in longer drives to work. While some alarmists fear that we are losing farmland in the process, a closer look reveals that most farmland converted to new uses is not being developed for housing or for commerce. Instead, most land formerly used in farming remains open land in the form of parks, forests, and pastures (Clue 3). While some new development is unsightly, not all of it harms the environment. Low density developments are often highly compatible with environmental quality. In fact, environmental quality is one of the benefits people seek, and are willing to pay for, in moving out into new areas (Clue 8).

LESSON 7
How Can Trading Emissions Rights Reduce Pollution?
In 1995, the Environmental Protection Agency reported that levels of six major air pollutants had decreased by 29 percent over the preceding 25 years. Much of the improvement could be attributed to government regulations, such as rules requiring the removal of lead from gasoline.

But that is not the whole story. Much recent improvement in air quality has been attained by means of an environmental program that relies on market forces. The government provides factories in a city with a specific number of pollution permits. A company then may discharge emissions up to the limit set in its permits, or it may sell some of its emissions allotment to other companies.

This plan actually allows some people to pollute more that others. How could selling pollution rights reduce pollution?

Clues 1, 3, and 8 are the most important for solving this mystery.

Solution
A system permitting trade in pollution rights begins with a target set by government as part of a larger effort to reduce overall levels of pollution (Clue 3). While government officials are good at identifying certain causes and levels of pollution, it is very difficult for them to know specifically what "clean actions" would provide the most effective responses by individual businesses. It is in respect to these particular decisions that the trading of emissions rights becomes critical. In a system that permits businesses to trade emissions rights, each company can determine for itself how best to address its emissions problems. A company producing emissions below its specified level might be willing to sell a portion of its emission rights to another company that could not otherwise meet its emission quotas except at a high cost that might threaten its continued existence (Clue 1). Buying these emission rights would still involve an added cost, however, and the company making the purchase would therefore have an incentive to begin addressing its emissions problem in a new manner (Clue 8). Moreover, because individual businesses possess the best information about the technology and procedures that will work best for them, they are in the best position to make choices that entail the lowest costs and the greatest benefits for them and their customers.

LESSON 8
Why Are Our National Parks Crumbling?
We love our National Parks. In fact, we may be loving them to death. U.S. National Park managers report all kinds of serious problems.

- Campgrounds are closed.
- Roads are crumbling.
- Buildings are in disrepair.
- Maintenance is years behind.

Yet many state parks, including those in Texas, South Dakota, and Arkansas, are offering new services to park users and are increasing their revenues.

Why are national parks crumbling while state parks are thriving?

Clues 4 and 6 are the most important for solving this mystery.

Solution
Officials responsible for managing and operating our National Parks have been hampered by the fact that they must depend on the U.S. Congress for the money they need to do their work (Clue 4). As park expenses have increased, Congress has failed to appropriate the funds the parks need to be successful. Congress also has restricted the authority of the parks' managers to generate new revenues. They have not been permitted to raise fees, charge fees for new programs, or market their natural attractions without permission from Washington.

State parks have been experimenting with a different approach to the revenue problem. State laws permit some state park managers to collect park fees and use those fees as they see fit for park maintenance and development. These laws have created an incentive for park managers to create new ways to serve the public while also improving the parks. The result has been an explosion of new services for state park users (Clue 6).

Some members of Congress have now begun to recognize that the incentive structure and the rules of the game need to be changed for the National Parks, too. In one recent experiment, for example, Congress permitted National Parks managers to increase park fees and charge new fees for special use permits, with the added revenue to be retained for park improvements.

CHAPTER 3

Contemporary Economic Mysteries

Chapter 3 presents the Visuals and Activity sheets you will need for lessons 1-16.

Each Visual includes one mystery, along with the *Handy Dandy Guide*. Each Activity sheet recaps the mystery and the *HDG*, for students' easy reference; each Activity sheet also presents clues and provides space in which students should write out their solutions.

The following mysteries are a potpourri of contemporary economic mysteries gleaned from news reports and various economics studies and reports.

CHAPTER 3, Lesson 1

Visual 1   The Case of the Pampered Chickens

Scientists are constantly looking for ways to improve our lives. They have little time to waste on nonsense. Yet a Texas A&M agricultural engineer has spent some of his time inventing a contact lens for chickens. Other scientists have experimented with playing classical music to barnyard animals.

Are these the stereotypical mad scientists? Why would scientists waste their time on contact lenses and Mozart for animals when so much really important work needs to be done?

Handy Dandy Guide
1. People *choose*.
2. People's choices involve *costs*.
3. People respond to *incentives* in predictable ways.
4. People create *economic systems* that influence individual choices and incentives.
5. People gain when they *trade* voluntarily.
6. People's choices have consequences that lie in the *future*.

CHAPTER 3, Lesson 1

Activity 1 The Case of the Pampered Chickens

Directions. Read the *Handy Dandy Guide* and the mystery. Read the clues assigned to your group. Be careful. While all the clues are correct, only some are *useful* in solving the mystery. Decide which clues are most relevant to solving the mystery. Use the clues and one or more of the ideas from the *Handy Dandy Guide* to figure out a solution to the mystery. Write your solution.

Handy Dandy Guide
1. People *choose*.
2. People's choices involve *costs*.
3. People respond to *incentives* in predictable ways.
4. People create *economic systems* that influence individual choices and incentives.
5. People gain when they *trade* voluntarily.
6. People's choices have consequences that lie in the *future*.

The Mystery
Scientists are constantly looking for ways to improve our lives. They have little time to waste on nonsense. Yet a Texas A&M agricultural engineer has spent some of his time inventing a contact lens for chickens. Other scientists have experimented with playing classical music to barnyard animals.

Are these the stereotypical mad scientists? Why would scientists waste their time with contact lenses for chickens or Mozart for animals when so much really important work needs to be done?

The Clues
1. Scientists receive billions of dollars to do agricultural research.
2. The United States government has a variety of programs to keep the price of some agricultural goods artificially high.
3. There is a scarcity of dollars to do scientific research.
4. Finding ways to lower the costs of agricultural production enables producers to earn higher profits while lowering prices for consumers.
5. American chickens produce millions of eggs each year.
6. The number of farms in the United States has been declining for several years—from 6.8 million in 1935 to less than 2 million today.
7. Satellites assist some farmers in providing information about the condition of their crops.
8. Farmers who are able to increase their efficiency and earn more profits benefit because they may keep most of what they earn by their efficiency.

Record your solution and explain it briefly here:

_____

_____

_____

_____

CHAPTER 3, Lesson 2

Visual 2   The Credit Card Mystery

Interest rates change. Yet interest rates on credit card balances remain high relative to other rates, often averaging around 17 percent. Several bills have been introduced in Congress to impose a nationwide ceiling on credit card interest rates.

Why do we have high interest rates on credit cards when other interest rates are so much lower?

Handy Dandy Guide
1. People *choose*.
2. People's choices involve *costs*.
3. People respond to *incentives* in predictable ways.
4. People create *economic systems* that influence individual choices and incentives.
5. People gain when they *trade* voluntarily.
6. People's choices have consequences that lie in the *future*.

CHAPTER 3, Lesson 2

Activity 2   The Credit Card Mystery

Directions. Read the *Handy Dandy Guide* and the mystery. Read the clues assigned to your group. Be careful. While all the clues are correct, only some are *useful* in solving the mystery. Decide which clues are most relevant to solving the mystery. Use the clues and one or more of the ideas from the *Handy Dandy Guide* to figure out a solution to the mystery. Write your solution.

Handy Dandy Guide
1. People *choose*.
2. People's choices involve *costs*.
3. People respond to *incentives* in predictable ways.
4. People create *economic systems* that influence individual choices and incentives.
5. People gain when they *trade* voluntarily.
6. People's choices have consequences that lie in the *future*.

The Mystery
Interest rates change. Yet interest rates on credit card balances remain high relative to other rates, often averaging around 17 percent. Several bills have been introduced in Congress to impose a nationwide ceiling on credit card interest rates.

Why do we have high interest rates on credit cards when other interest rates are so much lower?

The Clues
1. Many states have laws that place an interest rate ceiling on credit cards.
2. Consumers most often use credit cards to purchase consumable things like meals, clothing, and such.
3. Most loans are secured by collateral (cars and homes, for example). Most credit card loans are unsecured.
4. Credit cards provide a convenient way of obtaining a short-term loan.
5. Just over half of all Americans use credit cards.
6. Most credit cards have a credit limit.
7. Most credit cards have a grace period; if you pay off your balance in 30 days, you are not subject to finance charges.
8. Credit cards are issued by many institutions such as banks, department stores, and oil companies.
9. Levels of credit card theft and fraud are high.

Record your solution and explain it briefly here:

_____

_____

_____

_____

CHAPTER 3, Lesson 3

Visual 3   Unsafe at Any Level of Protection?

Cars today come loaded with safety equipment: padded dashboards, seat belts, collapsible steering columns, antilock brakes, air bags, and so forth.

But recent studies show that antilock braking systems are not reducing the number of accidents people suffer, or the cost of those accidents. Similarly, auto crash injuries have increased in number since cars have been equipped with air bags.

Why aren't safer cars producing fewer accidents?

Handy Dandy Guide
1. People *choose*.
2. People's choices involve *costs*.
3. People respond to *incentives* in predictable ways.
4. People create *economic systems* that influence individual choices and incentives.
5. People gain when they *trade* voluntarily.
6. People's choices have consequences that lie in the *future*.

CHAPTER 3, Lesson 3

Activity 3   Unsafe at Any Level of Protection?

Directions. Read the *Handy Dandy Guide* and the mystery. Read the clues assigned to your group. Be careful. While all the clues are correct, only some are *useful* in solving the mystery. Decide which clues are most relevant to solving the mystery. Use the clues and one or more of the ideas from the *Handy Dandy Guide* to figure out a solution to the mystery. Write your solution.

Handy Dandy Guide
1. People *choose*.
2. People's choices involve *costs*.
3. People respond to *incentives* in predictable ways.
4. People create *economic systems* that influence individual choices and incentives.
5. People gain when they *trade* voluntarily.
6. People's choices have consequences that lie in the *future*.

The Mystery
Cars today come loaded with safety equipment: padded dashboards, seat belts, collapsible steering columns, antilock brakes, air bags, and so forth.

But recent studies show that antilock braking systems are not reducing the number of accidents people suffer, or the cost of those accidents. Similarly, auto crash injuries have increased in number since cars have been equipped with airbags.

Why aren't safer cars producing fewer accidents?

The Clues
1. In 1965, Ralph Nader published a book entitled *Unsafe at Any Speed*.
2. The federal government has established many laws concerning how cars are to be made safe.
3. Some drivers will drive more aggressively when they are driving a car that is well equipped with safety features.
4. Most high school students complete courses in driver's training.
5. People are often in a hurry to get to their destinations.
6. Consumers pay more for cars with anti-lock brakes and airbags.
7. Motor vehicle crashes are a leading killer for people under 35 years of age.
8. The National Highway Traffic Safety Commission (NHTSC) is the federal agency responsible for reducing highway deaths, injuries, and property damage.
9. Sport utility vehicles continue to be popular with many Americans.

Record your solution and explain it briefly here:

_____

_____

_____

_____

CHAPTER 3, Lesson 4

Visual 4   Why Airborne Infants Aren't Required to Buckle Up

Infant airline passengers who ride in their own safety seats fly more safely than those who ride in their parents' laps.

Yet the U.S. government does not require the use of safety seats for infants. It has concluded that establishing such a rule would increase the number of infants killed in accidents while traveling.

Why wouldn't requiring safety seats save more babies?

Handy Dandy Guide
1. People *choose*.
2. People's choices involve *costs*.
3. People respond to *incentives* in predictable ways.
4. People create *economic systems* that influence individual choices and incentives.
5. People gain when they *trade* voluntarily.
6. People's choices have consequences that lie in the *future*.

CHAPTER 3, Lesson 4

Activity 4 Why Airborne Infants Aren't Required to Buckle Up

Directions. Read the *Handy Dandy Guide* and the mystery. Read the clues assigned to your group. Be careful. While all the clues are correct, only some are *useful* in solving the mystery. Decide which clues are most relevant to solving the mystery. Use the clues and one or more of the ideas from the *Handy Dandy Guide* to figure out a solution to the mystery. Write your solution.

Handy Dandy Guide
1. People *choose*.
2. People's choices involve *costs*.
3. People respond to *incentives* in predictable ways.
4. People create *economic systems* that influence individual choices and incentives.
5. People gain when they *trade* voluntarily.
6. People's choices have consequences that lie in the *future*.

The Mystery
Infant airline passengers who ride in their own safety seats fly more safely than those who ride in their parents' laps. Yet the U.S. government does not require the use of safety seats for infants. It has concluded that establishing such a rule would increase the number of infants killed in accidents while traveling.

Why wouldn't requiring safety seats save more babies?

The Clues
1. The Federal Aviation Administration in 1995 refused to require the use of safety seats for airborne infants.
2. In 1998, there were no air fatalities for United States-based air carriers.
3. Parents usually have to buy an extra ticket if they choose to use an infant safety seat, but not if the child travels seated in a parent's lap.
4. Travelers in automobiles are more likely to be involved in accidents than are travelers in airplanes.
5. The Federal Aviation Administration encourages voluntary use of safety seats for infants.
6. Airlines offer consumers special discounts to encourage people to fly at certain times.
7. The number of people flying has increased over the past 20 years.
8. Flight attendants have special training to handle most air emergencies.
9. Afternoon flights are more likely to be delayed than morning flights.

Record your solution and explain it briefly here:

_____

_____

_____

CHAPTER 3, Lesson 5

Visual 5   Having Many Children or Few

Most people eventually get married and have a family. But sometimes the number of children people decide to have is a puzzle. People in poor nations generally have more children than people in rich nations.

Why do people who can barely afford to pay for life's necessities have more children than people who are more affluent?

Handy Dandy Guide
1. People *choose*.
2. People's choices involve *costs*.
3. People respond to *incentives* in predictable ways.
4. People create *economic systems* that influence individual choices and incentives.
5. People gain when they *trade* voluntarily.
6. People's choices have consequences that lie in the *future*.

CHAPTER 3, Lesson 5

Activity 5   Having Many Children or Few

Directions. Read the *Handy Dandy Guide* and the mystery. Read the clues assigned to your group. Be careful. While all the clues are correct, only some are *useful* in solving the mystery. Decide which clues are most relevant to solving the mystery. Use the clues and one or more of the ideas from the *Handy Dandy Guide* to figure out a solution to the mystery. Write your solution.

Handy Dandy Guide
1. People *choose*.
2. People's choices involve *costs*.
3. People respond to *incentives* in predictable ways.
4. People create *economic systems* that influence individual choices and incentives.
5. People gain when they *trade* voluntarily.
6. People's choices have consequences that lie in the *future*.

The Mystery
Most people eventually get married and have a family. But sometimes the number of children people decide to have is a puzzle. People in poor nations generally have more children than people in rich nations.

Why do people who can barely pay for life's necessities have more children than people who are more affluent?

The Clues
1. Sub-Saharan Africa's population growth rates will be the highest of all major world regions for the next 25 years.
2. Women in nations like the United States generally have more economic opportunities than women have in Africa, Asia, and the Middle East.
3. Children in poor nations often work to contribute an income for their family.
4. At least 132 million births will occur every year for the next 25 years, despite falling fertility rates.
5. In 1996, 95 out of every 100 persons added to the world's population lived in less developed countries (LDCs).
6. College education is a big expense for families in developed nations like the United States.
7. Child labor laws often prevent children in developed nations from working legally.
8. The population of the world in the year 2000 is about 6 billion.
9. In developing countries today as compared with the 1960s, five times as many couples are using contraception.

Record your solution and explain it briefly here:

_____

_____

_____

CHAPTER 3, Lesson 6

Visual 6   Scarce Health Care in the Inner Cities

At a political rally, Senator Phogbound spoke eloquently about a complicated plan he had introduced to improve health care for low-income residents in America's inner cities and rural areas. The plan would cost billions of dollars.

As the Senator went on and on, a voice from the audience called out: "Ease up on our immigration restrictions, Senator, and more people will have access to health care!" Easing up on immigration restrictions would cost very little.

How could easing immigration rules help to provide health care for those who need it most?

Handy Dandy Guide
1. People *choose*.
2. People's choices involve *costs*.
3. People respond to *incentives* in predictable ways.
4. People create *economic systems* that influence individual choices and incentives.
5. People gain when they *trade* voluntarily.
6. People's choices have consequences that lie in the *future*.

CHAPTER 3, Lesson 6

Activity 6   Scarce Health Care in the Inner Cities

Directions. Read the *Handy Dandy Guide* and the mystery. Read the clues assigned to your group. Be careful. While all the clues are correct, only some are *useful* in solving the mystery. Decide which clues are most relevant to solving the mystery. Use the clues and one or more of the ideas from the *Handy Dandy Guide* to figure out a solution to the mystery. Write your solution.

Handy Dandy Guide
1. People *choose*.
2. People's choices involve *costs*.
3. People respond to *incentives* in predictable ways.
4. People create *economic systems* that influence individual choices and incentives.
5. People gain when they *trade* voluntarily.
6. People's choices have consequences that lie in the *future*.

The Mystery
At a political rally, Senator Phogbound spoke eloquently about a complicated plan he had introduced to improve health care for low-income residents in America's inner cities and rural areas. The plan would cost billions. As the Senator went on and on, a voice from the audience called out: "Ease up on our immigration restrictions, Senator, and more people will have access to health care!" Easing up on immigration restrictions would cost very little.

How could easing immigration rules help to provide health care to those who need it most?

The Clues
1. In 1997, the number of immigrants admitted for legal permanent residence in the United States was 798,378.
2. Many American physicians prefer to live and practice in suburban areas.
3. Legal immigration to the United States declined from 1996 to 1997.
4. In America's inner cities, many immigrants work as taxi cab drivers and as managers of convenience stores and low-cost motels.
5. It is legal for International Medical Graduates to practice medicine in the United States.
6. In 1997, over 5,000 physicians immigrated legally to the United States.
7. The United States Immigration & Naturalization Service is the federal agency that regulates immigration to the United States.
8. The Immigration Act of 1990 revised the numerical limits and preference categories used to regulate legal immigration.
9. Family-sponsored immigrants accounted for two thirds of all legal immigrants.

Record your solution and explain it briefly here:

_____

_____

_____

_____

CHAPTER 3, Lesson 7

Visual 7   Why Boris Couldn't Buy Much with His Rubles

The former Soviet Union was a super power in mineral wealth, military power, and space exploration.

Yet this strong and proud nation had difficulty producing simple, commonplace things—good shoes, for example, or good shirts, cars, bread, or French fries.

Why did a super power capable of building ICBMs not produce high quality consumer products?

Handy Dandy Guide
1. People *choose*.
2. People's choices involve *costs*.
3. People respond to *incentives* in predictable ways.
4. People create *economic systems* that influence individual choices and incentives.
5. People gain when they *trade* voluntarily.
6. People's choices have consequences that lie in the *future*.

CHAPTER 3, Lesson 7

Activity 7 Why Boris Couldn't Buy Much with His Rubles

Directions. Read the *Handy Dandy Guide* and the mystery. Read the clues assigned to your group. Be careful. While all the clues are correct, only some are *useful* in solving the mystery. Decide which clues are most relevant to solving the mystery. Use the clues and one or more of the ideas from the *Handy Dandy Guide* to figure out a solution to the mystery. Write your solution.

Handy Dandy Guide
1. People *choose*.
2. People's choices involve *costs*.
3. People respond to *incentives* in predictable ways.
4. People create *economic systems* that influence individual choices and incentives.
5. People gain when they *trade* voluntarily.
6. People's choices have consequences that lie in the *future*.

The Mystery
The former Soviet Union was a super power in mineral wealth, military power, and space exploration. Yet this strong and proud nation had difficulty producing simple, commonplace things—good shoes, for example, or good shirts, cars, bread, or French fries.

Why did a super power capable of producing ICBMs not produce high quality consumer products?

The Clues
1. The Soviet Union had a vast store of natural resources including timber, gold, and minerals of all sorts.
2. The Soviets strictly limited trade with the West.
3. The Soviets held several records in space exploration, including the first successful launch of an earth satellite.
4. Soviet enterprises did produce consumer products, but the products were often shoddy and in short supply.
5. The Soviets had vast reserves of oil.
6. In 1991, the Soviet Union collapsed.
7. The largest car manufacturing plant in the history of the auto industry was built in the Soviet Union.
8. The command form of economy established under Joseph Stalin offered few rewards to people who produced consumer goods.

Record your solution and explain it briefly here:

_____

_____

_____

_____

CHAPTER 3, Lesson 8

Visual 8   Why Would Mexico Want to Trade with the United States and Canada?

The people of Mexico are proud of their heritage, and they dislike outside interference in their affairs. Over the years Mexico has often been in conflict with its prosperous neighbor—the United States. Mexico and the United States have fought a war with each other, have had many border clashes, and have often disagreed about immigration and drug enforcement policies. Moreover, the two nations are economically different. Mexico has a relatively small economy, while the U.S. economy is the world's largest.

Mexico has joined the United States and Canada in agreements aimed at increasing trade among the three countries.

Why would a nation like Mexico, with a proud past and a small economy, want to increase trade with the United States—a former enemy with a larger economy?

Handy Dandy Guide
1. People *choose*.
2. People's choices involve *costs*.
3. People respond to *incentives* in predictable ways.
4. People create *economic systems* that influence individual choices and incentives.
5. People gain when they *trade* voluntarily.
6. People's choices have consequences that lie in the *future*.

CHAPTER 3, Lesson 8

Activity 8 Why Would Mexico Want to Trade with the United States and Canada?

Directions. Read the *Handy Dandy Guide* and the mystery. Read the clues assigned to your group. Be careful. While all the clues are correct, only some are *useful* in solving the mystery. Decide which clues are most relevant to solving the mystery. Use the clues and one or more of the ideas from the *Handy Dandy Guide* to figure out a solution to the mystery. Write your solution.

Handy Dandy Guide
1. People *choose*.
2. People's choices involve *costs*.
3. People respond to *incentives* in predictable ways.
4. People create *economic systems* that influence individual choices and incentives.
5. People gain when they *trade* voluntarily.
6. People's choices have consequences that lie in the *future*.

The Mystery
The people of Mexico are proud of their heritage, and they dislike outside interference in their affairs. Over the years Mexico has often been in conflict with its prosperous neighbor—the United States. Mexico and the United States have fought a war with each other, have had many border clashes, and have often disagreed about immigration and drug enforcement policies. Moreover, the two nations are economically different. Mexico has a relatively small economy, while the U.S. economy is the world's largest.

Mexico has joined the United States and Canada in agreements aimed at increasing trade among the three countries.

Why would a nation like Mexico, with a proud past and small economy, want to increase trade with the United States—a former enemy with a larger economy?

The Clues
1. Texas established its independence and became the Lone Star State in 1836.
2. Vegetable farmers in the United States do not welcome increased trade with Mexico.
3. Bankers in Mexico do not welcome increased trade with the United States.
4. The North American Free Trade Agreement (NAFTA) reduced many trade barriers among the United States, Canada, and Mexico.
5. Increased trade with the United States and Canada has increased the number of jobs in Mexico and helped to keep prices lower for consumers.
6. While U.S. trade increased with Mexico in the 1990s, U.S. unemployment rates hit 30-year lows.
7. Francisco (Pancho) Villa often clashed with the United States military.
8. The International Monetary Fund (IMF) often provides loans to nations like Mexico to assist with economic development.

Record your solution and explain it briefly here:

_____

_____

_____

_____

CHAPTER 3, Lesson 9

Visual 9   The Heart Throb Mystery

Every news stand sells magazines featuring glamorous, stylish people. Many Americans admire these attractive people. Some fantasize about meeting or dating the heart throbs of *People Magazine, Glamour, GQ,* and the rest.

Yet social scientists have found that people who are physically very attractive—those who seem most desirable—are less likely to marry than people whose appearance is more ordinary.

You might think the heart throbs would have suitors lined up outside their doors, eager for marriage. Why is this not so? What happens to the heart throbs on the way to the altar?

Handy Dandy Guide
1. People *choose*.
2. People's choices involve *costs*.
3. People respond to *incentives* in predictable ways.
4. People create *economic systems* that influence individual choices and incentives.
5. People gain when they *trade* voluntarily.
6. People's choices have consequences that lie in the *future*.

CHAPTER 3, Lesson 9

Activity 9 The Heart Throb Mystery

Directions. Read the *Handy Dandy Guide* and the mystery. Read the clues assigned to your group. Be careful. While all the clues are correct, only some are *useful* in solving the mystery. Decide which clues are most relevant to solving the mystery. Use the clues and one or more of the ideas from the *Handy Dandy Guide* to figure out a solution to the mystery. Write your solution.

Handy Dandy Guide
1. People *choose*.
2. People's choices involve *costs*.
3. People respond to *incentives* in predictable ways.
4. People create *economic systems* that influence individual choices and incentives.
5. People gain when they *trade* voluntarily.
6. People's choices have consequences that lie in the *future*.

The Mystery
Every news stand sells magazines featuring glamorous, stylish people. Many Americans admire these attractive people. Some fantasize about meeting or even dating the heart throbs of *People Magazine*, *Glamour*, *GQ*, and the rest.

Yet social scientists have found that people who are physically very attractive—those who seem most desirable—are less likely to marry than people whose appearance is more ordinary.

You might think the heart throbs would have suitors lined up outside their doors, eager for marriage. Why is this not so? What happens to the heart throbs on the way to the altar?

The Clues
1. Celebrities are often physically attractive.
2. Some men and women choose not to date highly attractive people because they know many other people are interested in such attractive individuals.
3. Attractive people often fear that individuals take an interest in them for their appearance rather than their character.
4. Some people fear that having a highly attractive spouse invites unwelcome advances from outsiders.
5. Today young people in the United States are marrying at later ages.
6. Married couples on average earn twice as much income as unmarried couples.
7. The typical wedding in the United States costs $12,000.
8. Support groups exist to assist unattractive people with issues related to self-esteem.

Record your solution and explain it briefly here:

_____

_____

_____

_____

CHAPTER 3, Lesson 10

Visual 10   The Gift-Giving Mystery: Why Not Just Send Money?

You don't have to be Midas or Scrooge to enjoy having money. Money is handy because individuals can exchange it for other things they want. Try getting a rental car or movie tickets on the barter system.

Yet most gift-givers don't give money. Instead they spend time trying to find the right gift, and they often get it wrong.

Why do people struggle to find special gifts for important days like birthdays and holidays when it would be easier and more efficient just to give money?

Handy Dandy Guide
1. People *choose*.
2. People's choices involve *costs*.
3. People respond to *incentives* in predictable ways.
4. People create *economic systems* that influence individual choices and incentives.
5. People gain when they *trade* voluntarily.
6. People's choices have consequences that lie in the *future*.

CHAPTER 3, Lesson 10

Activity 10   The Gift-Giving Mystery: Why Not Just Send Money?

Directions. Read the *Handy Dandy Guide* and the mystery. Read the clues assigned to your group. Be careful. While all the clues are correct, only some are *useful* in solving the mystery. Decide which clues are most relevant to solving the mystery. Use the clues and one or more of the ideas from the *Handy Dandy Guide* to figure out a solution to the mystery. Write your solution.

Handy Dandy Guide
1. People *choose*.
2. People's choices involve *costs*.
3. People respond to *incentives* in predictable ways.
4. People create *economic systems* that influence individual choices and incentives.
5. People gain when they *trade* voluntarily.
6. People's choices have consequences that lie in the *future*.

The Mystery
You don't have to be Midas or Scrooge to enjoy having money. Money is handy because people can exchange it for other things they want to have. Try getting a rental car or movie tickets on the barter system.

Yet most gift-givers don't give money. Instead they spend time trying to find the right gift, and they often get it wrong.

Why do people struggle to find special gifts for important days like birthdays and holidays when it would be easier and more efficient just to give money?

The Clues
1. Most department stores and gift shops offer gift certificates for that hard-to-please person on your gift list.
2. Prices traditionally increase prior to holidays and decrease afterward. More and more, however, retailers are offering sales in advance of major holidays.
3. Purchasing a special gift reflects thoughtfulness and caring on the part of the gift giver.
4. Many shoppers love large shopping malls and spend a great deal of time shopping in them.
5. As people age, their incomes ordinarily increase; as a result, they are often able to buy many of the things they wish to have. It can be challenging to shop for these people.
6. Gift-giving patterns vary with family traditions. Gift-giving customs are part of family culture.
7. People often give gifts of money to strangers—to paper carriers or waiters or waitresses.

Record your solution and explain it briefly here:

_____

_____

_____

_____

CHAPTER 3, Lesson 11

Visual 11   The Mystery of the Crazy Quilt Airfares

On a recent flight from Chicago to Tampa, Tim discovered that he had paid twice as much for his ticket as the woman seated beside him. Tim checked further, asking five other passengers about their tickets, and he found that each of the five had paid a different price. One person was flying "free" with frequent flier miles.

What is going on here? Why do different passengers pay different prices for exactly the same flight?

Handy Dandy Guide
1. People *choose*.
2. People's choices involve *costs*.
3. People respond to *incentives* in predictable ways.
4. People create *economic systems* that influence individual choices and incentives.
5. People gain when they *trade* voluntarily.
6. People's choices have consequences that lie in the *future*.

CHAPTER 3, Lesson 11

Activity 11   The Mystery of the Crazy Quilt Airfares

Directions. Read the *Handy Dandy Guide* and the mystery. Read the clues assigned to your group. Be careful. While all the clues are correct, only some are *useful* in solving the mystery. Decide which clues are most relevant to solving the mystery. Use the clues and one or more of the ideas from the *Handy Dandy Guide* to figure out a solution to the mystery. Write your solution.

Handy Dandy Guide
1. People *choose*.
2. People's choices involve *costs*.
3. People respond to *incentives* in predictable ways.
4. People create *economic systems* that influence individual choices and incentives.
5. People gain when they *trade* voluntarily.
6. People's choices have consequences that lie in the *future*.

The Mystery
On a recent flight from Chicago to Tampa, Tim discovered that he had paid twice as much for his ticket as the woman seated beside him. Tim checked further, asking five other passengers about their tickets, and he found that each of the five had paid a different price. One person was flying "free" with frequent flier miles.

What is going on here? Why do different passengers pay different prices for exactly the same flight?

The Clues
1. It is legal for airlines to charge different prices to different customers.
2. To some individuals, an air ticket to Tampa is worth more than it is to other individuals.
3. Record numbers of people today travel by air.
4. People earn frequent flyer points for more than just flying. Car rentals, hotels, and even credit cards offer frequent flyer miles.
5. Internet ticket auction companies have changed ticket pricing.
6. Frequent flyers often take advantage of special sales. Non-members often miss out on these opportunities.
7. Airplanes today often fly at near full capacity. In the past, half-empty planes were common.
8. Airports around the nation are spending more money to improve security.

Record your solution and explain it briefly here:

_____

_____

_____

_____

CHAPTER 3, Lesson 12

Visual 12 Why the Kid Who Skipped College Earns Big Bucks Playing Games

Many professional athletes never finish college. Some go directly into professional sports from high school. Yet professional athletes are frequently paid millions of dollars per year. Annual salaries for professional football players range from a few hundred thousand to several million dollars. The story is much the same among professional athletes in basketball and baseball.

Other people who perform worthy service—nurses, police officers, firefighters, and teachers—receive incomes far short of the amounts paid to professional athletes.

What is wrong with our values? Why are grown men and women paid millions of dollars to play kid games?

Handy Dandy Guide
1. People *choose*.
2. People's choices involve *costs*.
3. People respond to *incentives* in predictable ways.
4. People create *economic systems* that influence individual choices and incentives.
5. People gain when they *trade* voluntarily.
6. People's choices have consequences that lie in the *future*.

CHAPTER 3, Lesson 12

Activity 12   Why the Kid Who Skipped College Earns Big Bucks Playing Games

Directions. Read the *Handy Dandy Guide* and the mystery. Read the clues assigned to your group. Be careful. While all the clues are correct, only some are *useful* in solving the mystery. Decide which clues are most relevant to solving the mystery. Use the clues and one or more of the ideas from the *Handy Dandy Guide* to figure out a solution to the mystery. Write your solution.

Handy Dandy Guide
1. People *choose*.
2. People's choices involve *costs*.
3. People respond to *incentives* in predictable ways.
4. People create *economic systems* that influence individual choices and incentives.
5. People gain when they *trade* voluntarily.
6. People's choices have consequences that lie in the *future*.

The Mystery
Many professional athletes never finish college. Some go directly into professional sports from high school. Yet professional athletes are frequently paid millions of dollars per year. Annual salaries for professional football players range from a few hundred thousand to several million dollars. The story is much the same among professional athletes in basketball and baseball.

Yet other people who perform worthy service—nurses, police officers, firefighters, and teachers—receive incomes far short of the amounts paid to professional athletes.

What is wrong with our values? Why are grown men and women paid millions of dollars to play kid games?

The Clues
1. In addition to their salaries, athletes often earn money through endorsements, speaking engagements, signing autographs, and so forth.
2. Few people possess the skills needed to throw big league fast balls, deliver one-handed jams, and toss game-winning touchdown passes.
3. Most professional athletes have gone to college.
4. Coaches encourage competition among their players as a way to bring out their best performance.
5. Fans pay to see professional athletes perform in person; they also tune in by the millions to watch athletes on television.
6. A recent strike by professional baseball players was a turn-off for many fans.
7. Like police officers and firefighters, professional athletes risk serious injury.
8. The non-labor costs of running a team—uniforms, equipment, air fares—have been increasing recently.

Record your solution and explain it briefly here:

_____

_____

_____

_____

CHAPTER 3, Lesson 13

Visual 13   What's in a Name?

Many consumers love to buy brand name products. They enjoy the quality of the products at the price they pay.

But wait a minute. Why buy Hallmark Cards, Ivory Soap, Coca Cola, or Wheaties? Consumer advocates tell us that many non-brand name products—such as store brands—are nearly identical to their brand name rivals and almost always cost much less.

Why don't more cost-conscious consumers ignore all the brand name hype and save money by buying the store brand?

Handy Dandy Guide
1. People *choose*.
2. People's choices involve *costs*.
3. People respond to *incentives* in predictable ways.
4. People create *economic systems* that influence individual choices and incentives.
5. People gain when they *trade* voluntarily.
6. People's choices have consequences that lie in the *future*.

CHAPTER 3, Lesson 13

Activity 13   What's in a Name?

Directions. Read the *Handy Dandy Guide* and the mystery. Read the clues assigned to your group. Be careful. While all the clues are correct, only some are *useful* in solving the mystery. Decide which clues are most relevant to solving the mystery. Use the clues and one or more of the ideas from the *Handy Dandy Guide* to figure out a solution to the mystery. Write your solution.

Handy Dandy Guide
1. People *choose*.
2. People's choices involve *costs*.
3. People respond to *incentives* in predictable ways.
4. People create *economic systems* that influence individual choices and incentives.
5. People gain when they *trade* voluntarily.
6. People's choices have consequences that lie in the *future*.

The Mystery
Many consumers love to buy brand name products. They enjoy the quality of the products at the price they pay.

But wait a minute. Why buy Hallmark Cards, Ivory Soap, Coca Cola, or Wheaties? Consumer advocates tell us that many non-brand name products—such as store brands—are nearly identical to their brand name rivals and almost always cost much less.

Why don't cost conscious consumers ignore all the brand name hype and save money by buying the store brand?

The Clues
1. Brand name products often cost more because brand name producers spend so much money on advertising.
2. Store brand products are usually displayed in easy view for customers to find, just like the brand name products.
3. Brand name products are often endorsed by famous athletes or celebrities.
4. Experimenting with store brand products does cost consumers something.
5. Producers of brand name products take pride in delivering consistent, predictable quality.
6. Clever advertising of a brand name product can often attract a first-time buyer.
7. Some experiments by brand name producers fail. Remember the new Coke?
8. Reductions in tariffs have increased imports of no-name products.

Record your solution and explain it briefly here:

_____

_____

_____

_____

CHAPTER 3, Lesson 14

Visual 14 Why Don't All Students Study Hard at School?

Most people know that higher levels of formal education go along, on average, with higher incomes for both men and women. People who complete high school, for example, earn more income than people who do not. People who complete a year or two of college earn more than people who do not. People who complete a college degree earn more than do those who do not.

Yet many high school students seem to care little about their education. Many choose not to study very hard. Some even drop out of school.

Since the link between education and income is well established, why do some high school students disdain education?

Handy Dandy Guide
1. People *choose*.
2. People's choices involve *costs*.
3. People respond to *incentives* in predictable ways.
4. People create *economic systems* that influence individual choices and incentives.
5. People gain when they *trade* voluntarily.
6. People's choices have consequences that lie in the *future*.

CHAPTER 3, Lesson 14

Activity 14 Why Don't All Students Study Hard at School?

Directions. Read the *Handy Dandy Guide* and the mystery. Read the clues assigned to your group. Be careful. While all the clues are correct, only some are *useful* in solving the mystery. Decide which clues are most relevant to solving the mystery. Use the clues and one or more of the ideas from the *Handy Dandy Guide* to figure out a solution to the mystery. Write your solution.

Handy Dandy Guide
1. People *choose*.
2. People's choices involve *costs*.
3. People respond to *incentives* in predictable ways.
4. People create *economic systems* that influence individual choices and incentives.
5. People gain when they *trade* voluntarily.
6. People's choices have consequences that lie in the *future*.

The Mystery
Most people know that higher levels of formal education go along, on average, with higher incomes for both men and women. People who complete high school, for example, earn more income than people who do not. People who complete a year or two of college earn more than those who do not. People who complete a college degree earn more than those who do not.

Yet many high school students seem to care very little about their education. Many choose not to study very hard. Some even drop out of school.

Since the link between education and income is well established, why do some high school students disdain education?

The Clues
1. High school students in Europe spend more time reading than American students do.
2. A public opinion poll revealed that many high school students said that they could study harder in school.
3. Many high school students work at part-time jobs.
4. Some American high school students do study hard and perform at high levels.
5. The direct cost of going to college—tuition, board, and books—has been increasing.
6. Many high school students will be admitted to college despite mediocre grades.
7. Working harder—increasing study time, attending class regularly, doing homework—almost always results in improved grades.
8. Employers rarely request high school transcripts or attendance records.

Record your solution and explain it briefly here:

_____

_____

_____

CHAPTER 3, Lesson 15

Visual 15   Where Did the ATMs Come From?

Automated teller machines (ATMs) are nearly everywhere. It is hard to pump gas or visit a convenience store and not be reminded of how easy it is to get cash or make a bank transaction.

Even people living in rural areas, places where ATMs were not to be found until the 1990s, now have easy access to cash and other services through the ubiquitous ATMs.

Where did all the ATMs come from? How is it that, almost overnight, ATMs have popped up everywhere—even in small towns like Townsend, Wisconsin, population 500?

Handy Dandy Guide
1. People *choose*.
2. People's choices involve *costs*.
3. People respond to *incentives* in predictable ways.
4. People create *economic systems* that influence individual choices and incentives.
5. People gain when they *trade* voluntarily.
6. People's choices have consequences that lie in the *future*.

CHAPTER 3, Lesson 15

Activity 15   Where Did the ATMs Come From?

Directions. Read the *Handy Dandy Guide* and the mystery. Read the clues assigned to your group. Be careful. While all the clues are correct, only some are *useful* in solving the mystery. Decide which clues are most relevant to solving the mystery. Use the clues and one or more of the ideas from the *Handy Dandy Guide* to figure out a solution to the mystery. Write your solution.

Handy Dandy Guide
1. People *choose*.
2. People's choices involve *costs*.
3. People respond to *incentives* in predictable ways.
4. People create *economic systems* that influence individual choices and incentives.
5. People gain when they *trade* voluntarily.
6. People's choices have consequences that lie in the *future*.

The Mystery
Automated teller machines (ATMs) are nearly everywhere. It is hard to pump gas or visit a convenience store and not be reminded of how easy it is to get cash or make a bank transaction.

Even people living in rural areas, places where ATMs were not to be found until the 1990s, now have easy access to cash and other services through the ubiquitous ATMs.

Where did all the ATMs come from? How is it that, almost overnight, ATMs have popped up everywhere—even in small towns like Townsend, Wisconsin, population 500?

The Clues
1. Banks that provide ATMs do not charge their customers for ATM use. However, many banks do charge for ATM use by people who are not their customers. Fees range from $1 to $2.50 or more.
2. Some politicians want to prohibit banks from charging fees for the use of ATMs by people who aren't bank customers.
3. The number of ATMs skyrocketed when ATM networks began to charge fees to non-customers of the ATM owner.
4. Many Americans dislike paying ATM fees to gain access to their cash.
5. When banks began charging fees to non-customers for the use of ATMs, it significantly reduced the number of transactions required per month for the ATM to turn a profit.
6. Several consumer groups have banded together with political leaders in an effort to ban ATM fees.
7. Between 1991 and 1995, financial institutions lost an average of more than $10,000 per ATM machine per year.

Record your solution and explain it briefly here:

_____

_____

_____

===== CHAPTER 3, Lesson 16 =====

Visual 16 Why Everything but the Kitchen Sink Gets Stashed in the Overhead Luggage Bins on Airplanes

Airlines periodically clamp down on people who try to pass off small pianos or lawn mowers as carry-on luggage. It is easy to understand why the airlines get worried. Some passengers try to carry everything from banjos to lobster crates on board their flights. The heavy, awkward bags they stuff into the overhead luggage bins can be downright dangerous as they shift around during the flight or fall down on unsuspecting passengers when the compartment doors are opened.

But perhaps the passengers are not to blame. After all, if they check their luggage they incur some risk of losing it or having to wait a long time for it to show up at the luggage carousel. They also incur a risk of breakage or theft of valuable items.

To date, the solution proposed by the airlines is to do a better job of enforcing their rules about size-limits for carry-on bags.

In an industry sophisticated enough to cope with astrophysics, schedules coordinated across multiple time zones, the vagaries of complex weather systems, and the mysteries of the microwaved omelette, is there really no good way to solve the on-board luggage problem? Can you use economic thinking to do better?

Handy Dandy Guide
1. People *choose*.
2. People's choices involve *costs*.
3. People respond to *incentives* in predictable ways.
4. People create *economic systems* that influence individual choices and incentives.
5. People gain when they *trade* voluntarily.
6. People's choices have consequences that lie in the *future*.

CHAPTER 3, Lesson 16

Activity 16 Why Everything but the Kitchen Sink Gets Stashed in the Overhead Luggage Bins on Airplanes

Directions. Read the *Handy Dandy Guide* and the mystery. Read the clues assigned to your group. Be careful. While all the clues are correct, only some are *useful* in solving the mystery. Decide which clues are most relevant to solving the mystery. Use the clues and one or more of the ideas from the *Handy Dandy Guide* to figure out a solution to the mystery. Write your solution.

Handy Dandy Guide
1. People *choose*.
2. People's choices involve *costs*.
3. People respond to *incentives* in predictable ways.
4. People create *economic systems* that influence individual choices and incentives.
5. People gain when they *trade* voluntarily.
6. People's choices have consequences that lie in the *future*.

The Mystery
Airlines periodically clamp down on people who try to pass off small pianos or lawn mowers as carry-on luggage. It is easy to understand why the airlines get worried. Some passengers try to carry everything from banjos to lobster crates on board their flights. The heavy, awkward bags they stuff into the overhead luggage bins can be downright dangerous as they shift around during the flight or fall down on unsuspecting passengers when the compartment doors are opened.

But perhaps the passengers are not to blame. After all, if they check their luggage they incur a risk of losing it or having to wait a long time for it to show up at the luggage carousel. They also incur a risk of breakage or theft of valuable items.

To date, the solution proposed by the airlines is to do a better job of enforcing their rules about size-limits for carry-on bags.

In an industry sophisticated enough to deal with astrophysics, the coordination of schedules across multiple time zones, the vagaries of complex weather systems, and the mysteries of the microwaved omelette, is there really no good way to solve the on-board luggage problem? Can you use economic thinking to do better?

The Clues
1. Today, thanks to the new global economy, international air travel is growing faster than domestic air travel.
2. The Airline Deregulation Act of 1978 phased out federal control of airlines, in order to promote industry competition.
3. Some airline safety experts suggest that (because of the dangers created by falling luggage) airline passengers should be encouraged to wear protective helmets.
4. Many airlines have reduced the number of scheduled flights they offer and have come forward with special promotional deals in order to keep their planes full.
5. The problem with overheard luggage bins is that a passenger cannot purchase the right to use the storage space in the compartment above his or her seat.
6. Newer planes offer more space for carry-on bags than the older planes did.
7. Air travel was once considered a perk for the wealthy. Now it is a common mode of travel.
8. Major corporations have recently eliminated 1.5 million middle-and upper-management positions, sparking a corresponding decrease in business travel.

Record your solution and explain it briefly here:

_____

_____

_____

CHAPTER 4

Public Choice Mysteries

Chapter 4 presents the Visuals and Activity sheets you will need for lessons 1-11.

Each Visual includes one mystery, along with the *Handy Dandy Guide*. Each Activity sheet recaps the mystery and the *HDG*, for students' easy reference; each Activity sheet also presents clues and provides space in which students should write out their solutions.

Each of the mysteries in Chapter 4 reflects a set of ideas referred to as public choice theory. The following paragraphs offer a description of the basic tenets of public choice theory for teachers who would like to have a brief refresher.

The study of economics ordinarily focuses on the marketplace. However, economists in recent years have also used the assumptions of economics to obtain new insights into many so-called nonmarket phenomena such as marriage, divorce, fertility, health, education, and crime. The behavior of people in government can also be studied in this fashion.

The application of economic analysis to the study of government is often referred to as public choice theory. Public choice analysis emphasizes the point that individual behavior in government is influenced by many of the same considerations that influence individual behavior in markets.

Monetary rewards certainly play a role in influencing the decisions of people in private or public life. But public choice theory recognizes many incentives in addition to monetary rewards. People obviously respond to a wide range of incentives related to family, recognition, leisure, travel, information, and personal satisfaction derived from community service. Because such incentives often influence political leaders, we can forecast the actions they might take.

Closely related to the idea that incentives influence behavior is the notion that political leaders, like other people, measure additional costs against additional benefits as they make decisions. For example, individuals who consider running for political office may assess the trade-offs, weighing the additional burdens of less time with family and less time working at their chosen profession against the additional benefits of satisfaction gained through additional community service and an increased sense of recognition and power. Thus, in the parlance of economics, political leaders make marginal decisions.

Another similarity between behaviors in the private sector and the public sector is that both involve competition. The competition in each sector is driven by scarcity. Consider the example of the first-time seeker of public office. First, nomination slots are scarce; competition is needed to win the nomination from opponents. Then there is competition in earning contributions and attracting volunteers (scarce resources) to work on the campaign. Finally, there is the direct competition to win the support of the voters. Of course, the victorious candidate must subsequently compete to find office space, the best staff possible, and to gain the support of colleagues for policies favored during the campaign. Competition in government is not limited to elected officials. Non-elected agency heads compete for increased budgets and authority. Public sector employees are often in competition with others who seek to improve their equipment, gain power, attain promotions, or increase their salaries.

Public choice theory—with its stress on incentives, scarcity, and competition—explains events that otherwise might seem mysterious or contradictory. For example, application of choice theory can help explain why politicians sometimes must choose between winning elections and advocating or providing good government policy. Public choice theory also helps explain why politicians may favor large budget deficits even when they know that such deficits hurt the economy. And it helps explain how a special interest group, which benefits a small number of constituents, can decisively influence legislation that benefits only a few while imposing a relatively small cost on many.

CHAPTER 4, Lesson 1

Visual 1   The Electoral College Mystery

In the American system of government, majority rule is a fundamental principle of democracy.

Yet in presidential elections we continue to use the Electoral College—an undemocratic institution. Under some circumstances, Electoral College procedures permit the election of a candidate who has not earned a majority of the national popular vote.

Why does the world's greatest democracy tolerate such an undemocratic institution?

Handy Dandy Guide
1. People *choose*.
2. People's choices involve *costs*.
3. People respond to *incentives* in predictable ways.
4. People create *economic systems* that influence individual choices and incentives.
5. People gain when they *trade* voluntarily.
6. People's choices have consequences that lie in the *future*.

CHAPTER 4, Lesson 1

Activity 1 The Electoral College Mystery

Directions. Read the *Handy Dandy Guide* and the mystery. Read the clues assigned to your group. Be careful. While all the clues are correct, only some are *useful* in solving the mystery. Decide which clues are most relevant to solving the mystery. Use the clues and one or more of the ideas from the *Handy Dandy Guide* to figure out a solution to the mystery. Write your solution.

Handy Dandy Guide
1. People *choose*.
2. People's choices involve *costs*.
3. People respond to *incentives* in predictable ways.
4. People create *economic systems* that influence individual choices and incentives.
5. People gain when they *trade* voluntarily.
6. People's choices have consequences that lie in the *future*.

The Mystery
In the American system of government, majority rule is a fundamental principle of democracy. Yet in presidential elections we continue to use the Electoral College—an undemocratic institution. Under some circumstances, Electoral College procedures permit the election of a candidate who has not earned a majority of the national popular vote.

Why does the world's greatest democracy tolerate such an undemocratic institution?

The Clues
1. Amending the U.S. Constitution requires the approval of three fourths of the states.
2. The number of representatives a state may send to the U.S. House of Representatives is determined by the state's population. More people, more representatives.
3. Each state elects two U.S. senators, regardless of population.
4. The electors from each state who make up the Electoral College are usually selected in a "winner take all" manner. If the Vegetarian Party wins 51 percent of the vote in Texas, the Vegetarians get to cast all 29 of Texas's electoral votes.
5. In 1824, 1876, 1888, and 1992, the winner of the U.S. presidential election did not receive a majority of the popular vote.
6. A victorious president wishes to say that the election represents a mandate.
7. An incumbent is someone who already holds office.
8. Each state is allotted by the Constitution as many electoral votes as it has senators and representatives in Congress. Thus no state has fewer than three electoral votes.
9. A political action committee (PAC) is a legal committee used in presidential fund-raising.

Record your solution and explain it briefly here:

_____

_____

_____

_____

CHAPTER 4, Lesson 2

Visual 2 Where Did the Mortgages Go?

In the 1970s, a law in the state of Illinois prohibited lenders from charging more than 8 percent interest on home mortgages. The purpose of this law was to make home-buying more affordable for people earning low incomes. However, by the mid-1970s, in a period of rising interest rates, people wanting to buy homes in Illinois found it almost impossible to get home loans from state bankers.

This seems odd. People who lend money can't make any money themselves unless they issue loans.

What happened to the mortgages in Illinois? Why did people in the money-lending business not want to lend money?

Handy Dandy Guide
1. People *choose*.
2. People's choices involve *costs*.
3. People respond to *incentives* in predictable ways.
4. People create *economic systems* that influence individual choices and incentives.
5. People gain when they *trade* voluntarily.
6. People's choices have consequences that lie in the *future*.

CHAPTER 4, Lesson 2

Activity 2 Where Did the Mortgages Go?

Directions. Read the *Handy Dandy Guide* and the mystery. Read the clues assigned to your group. Be careful. While all the clues are correct, only some are *useful* in solving the mystery. Decide which clues are most relevant to solving the mystery. Use the clues and one or more of the ideas from the *Handy Dandy Guide* to figure out a solution to the mystery. Write your solution.

Handy Dandy Guide
1. People *choose*.
2. People's choices involve *costs*.
3. People respond to *incentives* in predictable ways.
4. People create *economic systems* that influence individual choices and incentives.
5. People gain when they *trade* voluntarily.
6. People's choices have consequences that lie in the *future*.

The Mystery
In the 1970s, a law in the state of Illinois prohibited lenders from charging more than 8 percent interest on home mortgages. The purpose of this law was to make home-buying more affordable for people earning low incomes. However, by the mid-1970s, people wanting to buy homes in Illinois found it almost impossible to get home loans from state bankers.

This seems odd. People who lend money can't make any money themselves unless they issue loans.

What happened to the mortgages in Illinois? Why did people in the money lending business not want to issue loans?

The Clues
1. Banks are businesses.
2. In issuing loans, banks strive to make a profit by charging higher interest rates than the rates they pay to depositors.
3. State and federal agencies regulate banks.
4. Usury laws set limits on the interest rates lenders are permitted to charge. Sometimes usury laws require lenders to charge less than current market rates of interest.
5. The Federal Reserve is the central bank of the United States.
6. The Federal Deposit Insurance Corporation guarantees the deposits of bank customers, up to a set limit.
7. The 1970s were a time of rising interest rates and rising inflation.
8. Savings and loan institutions and credit unions provide many of the same services as commercial banks.
9. Banks are required to keep only a fraction of their deposits in the form of reserves.

Record your solution and explain it briefly here:

_____

_____

_____

_____

CHAPTER 4, Lesson 3

Visual 3 The Mystery of the Politicians Who Can't Say No

During the 1980s, the U.S. federal government approved spending levels that created huge federal budget deficits.

Most economists agree that these large deficits caused or aggravated many economic problems, pushing inflation and interest rates up.

Why would government leaders approve levels of spending that they knew would hurt the economy.

Handy Dandy Guide
1. People *choose*.
2. People's choices involve *costs*.
3. People respond to *incentives* in predictable ways.
4. People create *economic systems* that influence individual choices and incentives.
5. People gain when they *trade* voluntarily.
6. People's choices have consequences that lie in the *future*.

CHAPTER 3, Lesson 3

Activity 3 The Mystery of the Politicians Who Can't Say No

Directions. Read the *Handy Dandy Guide* and the mystery. Read the clues assigned to your group. Be careful. While all the clues are correct, only some are *useful* in solving the mystery. Decide which clues are most relevant to solving the mystery. Use the clues and one or more of the ideas from the *Handy Dandy Guide* to figure out a solution to the mystery. Write your solution.

Handy Dandy Guide
1. People *choose*.
2. People's choices involve *costs*.
3. People respond to *incentives* in predictable ways.
4. People create *economic systems* that influence individual choices and incentives.
5. People gain when they *trade* voluntarily.
6. People's choices have consequences that lie in the *future*.

The Mystery
During the 1980s, the U.S. federal government approved spending levels that created huge federal budget deficits. Most economists agree that these large deficits caused many economic problems, pushing inflation and interest rates up.

Why would government leaders approve levels of spending that they know hurt the economy?

The Clues
1. Most politicians who hold elected office want to be re-elected; they have an obvious incentive to seek votes.
2. Politicians are rewarded by interest groups and voters when they bring federal spending projects—roads, dams, business contracts—to their home district or state.
3. To win the presidency, a candidate must win a majority of votes in the Electoral College.
4. In seeking votes and campaign funds, politicians face competition.
5. During their campaigns, politicians often depend upon glittering generalities, earnestly but vaguely insisting, for example, that they believe in a system of fair taxes, or fiscal responsibility.
6. People between ages 18 to 24 are the least likely to vote.
7. The average U.S federal deficit in the 1980s was about $170 billion.
8. The U.S. federal debt as of 1999 was $6 trillion.
9. Interest groups—dairy farmers, steel producers, trial lawyers, and so on—that help to raise campaign funds for politicians also make special efforts to inform politicians about their special problems.

Record your solution and explain it briefly here:

_____

_____

_____

_____

CHAPTER 4, Lesson 4

Visual 4   Is Parking Really Free in Fargo?

In a gesture aimed at banishing an annoyance familiar to people who live in big cities, North Dakota legislators voted in 1999 to retain the state's ban on parking meters. One state senator said that local government shouldn't be able to collect money for parking on public streets. Like driving on public roads, parking on public streets should be free.

This sounds too good to be true. Why don't cities and states everywhere provide free parking?

Maybe it is too good to be true. Is parking really free in Fargo?

Handy Dandy Guide
1. People *choose*.
2. People's choices involve *costs*.
3. People respond to *incentives* in predictable ways.
4. People create *economic systems* that influence individual choices and incentives.
5. People gain when they *trade* voluntarily.
6. People's choices have consequences that lie in the *future*.

CHAPTER 4, Lesson 4

Activity 4   Is Parking Really Free in Fargo?

Directions. Read the *Handy Dandy Guide* and the mystery. Read the clues assigned to your group. Be careful. While all the clues are correct, only some are *useful* in solving the mystery. Decide which clues are most relevant to solving the mystery. Use the clues and one or more of the ideas from the *Handy Dandy Guide* to figure out a solution to the mystery. Write your solution.

Handy Dandy Guide
1. People *choose*.
2. People's choices involve *costs*.
3. People respond to *incentives* in predictable ways.
4. People create *economic systems* that influence individual choices and incentives.
5. People gain when they *trade* voluntarily.
6. People's choices have consequences that lie in the *future*.

The Mystery
In a gesture aimed at banishing an annoyance familiar to people who live in big cities, North Dakota legislators voted in 1999 to retain the state's ban on parking meters. One state senator said that local government shouldn't be able to collect money for parking on public streets. Like driving on public roads, parking on public streets should be free. This sounds too good to be true. Why don't cities and states everywhere guarantee free parking?

Maybe it is too good to be true. Is parking really free in Fargo?

The Clues
1. On the Fourth of July, many small towns prohibit curbside parking on Main Street in order to free up space for the Fourth of July parade.
2. North Dakota is the 17th largest state in the United States.
3. Fargo is the largest city in North Dakota, with a population of 77,052 people.
4. The Western Meadowlark is North Dakota's state bird.
5. Milk is North Dakota's state beverage.
6. North Dakota has more road area per acre of land than any other state.
7. North Dakota has more registered vehicles than it has residents.
8. Land area used for outdoor cafes can't be used (at the same time, at least) for roadway expansion.
9. North Dakota has three Congressional seats—two senators and one representative.

Record your solution and explain it briefly here:

_____

_____

_____

_____

CHAPTER 4, Lesson 5

Visual 5 The Mystery of the Missing Pubs

Pubs are central to social life in Ireland. They serve as social centers for neighborhoods, providing people with places to meet for business and pleasure.

Ireland in the 1990s has had a strong economy. The "Celtic Tiger" is the envy of Europe.

Given the attachment of many Irish people to the pubs, and given the recent strength of Ireland's economy, you might suppose you could find a pub on every street corner in Irish towns and cities. But generally this is not so. Even in Dublin, there are some neighborhoods with only a handful of pubs to serve thousands of people.

Why are there so few pubs in Dublin?

Handy Dandy Guide
1. People *choose*.
2. People's choices involve *costs*.
3. People respond to *incentives* in predictable ways.
4. People create *economic systems* that influence individual choices and incentives.
5. People gain when they *trade* voluntarily.
6. People's choices have consequences that lie in the *future*.

CHAPTER 4, Lesson 5

Activity 5   The Mystery of the Missing Pubs

Directions. Read the *Handy Dandy Guide* and the mystery. Read the clues assigned to your group. Be careful. While all the clues are correct, only some are *useful* in solving the mystery. Decide which clues are most relevant to solving the mystery. Use the clues and one or more of the ideas from the *Handy Dandy Guide* to figure out a solution to the mystery. Write your solution.

Handy Dandy Guide
1. People *choose*.
2. People's choices involve *costs*.
3. People respond to *incentives* in predictable ways.
4. People create *economic systems* that influence individual choices and incentives.
5. People gain when they *trade* voluntarily.
6. People's choices have consequences that lie in the *future*.

The Mystery
Pubs are central to social life in Ireland. They serve as social centers for neighborhoods, providing people with places to meet for business and pleasure.

Ireland in the 1990s has had a strong economy. The "Celtic Tiger" is the envy of Europe. Given the attachment of many Irish people to the pubs, and given the recent strength of Ireland's economy, you might suppose you could find a pub on every corner in Irish towns and cities. But generally this is not so. Even in Dublin, there are some neighborhoods with only a handful of pubs to serve thousands of people.

Why are there so few pubs in Dublin?

The Clues
1. Ireland has a population of just over 3.6 million people.
2. The population of Ireland is 93 percent Roman Catholic.
3. Ireland has 26 counties.
4. In 1902, a law aimed at reducing drinking was passed in Ireland; it limited the number of pub licenses at the level then in existence.
5. In 1997, Ireland's Real Gross Domestic Product increased by 6 percent.
6. Over 40 percent of the Irish population resides within 60 miles of Dublin.
7. In 1902, a law was enacted which barred the transfer of pub licenses across county lines.
8. A 1960s law prohibits building new pubs within one mile of an existing pub (in rural areas).
9. Pub owners in Ireland have an organization that has fought efforts to change the old laws and permit licenses for new pubs to be issued.

Record your solution and explain it briefly here:

_____

_____

_____

_____

CHAPTER 4, Lesson 6

Visual 6 How We Almost Got a Sixth Great Lake

Every school student knows there are five Great Lakes. They remember the lakes easily by recalling "HOMES," the letters of which stand for Lake *H*uron, Lake *O*ntario, Lake *M*ichigan, Lake *E*rie, and Lake *S*uperior. This is common knowledge.

Yet, Mr. Patrick Leahy, a United States Senator from Vermont, believes that Lake Champlain, which borders Vermont, New York, and Canada, is also a Great Lake. "Vermonters have always considered Lake Champlain the sixth Great Lake," he declared in 1998. Then he undertook an effort to have Lake Champlain officially designated as a Great Lake.

Why would a respected U.S. Senator think there are six Great Lakes, when school children know that is not true?

Handy Dandy Guide
1. People *choose*.
2. People's choices involve *costs*.
3. People respond to *incentives* in predictable ways.
4. People create *economic systems* that influence individual choices and incentives.
5. People gain when they *trade* voluntarily.
6. People's choices have consequences that lie in the *future*.

CHAPTER 4, Lesson 6

Activity 6 How We Almost Got a Sixth Great Lake

Directions. Read the *Handy Dandy Guide* and the mystery. Read the clues assigned to your group. Be careful. While all the clues are correct, only some are *useful* in solving the mystery. Decide which clues are most relevant to solving the mystery. Use the clues and one or more of the ideas from the *Handy Dandy Guide* to figure out a solution to the mystery. Write your solution.

Handy Dandy Guide
1. People *choose*.
2. People's choices involve *costs*.
3. People respond to *incentives* in predictable ways.
4. People create *economic systems* that influence individual choices and incentives.
5. People gain when they *trade* voluntarily.
6. People's choices have consequences that lie in the *future*.

The Mystery
Every school student knows there are five Great Lakes. They remember the lakes easily by recalling "HOMES," the letters of which stand for Lake *H*uron, Lake *O*ntario, Lake *M*ichigan, Lake *E*rie, and Lake *S*uperior. This is common knowledge. Yet, Mr. Patrick Leahy, a United States Senator from Vermont, believes that Lake Champlain, which borders Vermont, New York, and Canada, is also a Great Lake. "Vermonters have always considered Lake Champlain the sixth Great Lake," he declared in 1998. Then he undertook an effort to have Lake Champlain officially designated as a Great Lake.

Why would a U.S. Senator think there are six Great Lakes when school children know that is not true?

The Clues
1. Lake Superior is the largest of the Great Lakes.
2. An Indian name for Lake Michigan was "Michi gami."
3. Lake Superior has the largest surface area of any freshwater lake in the world.
4. Lake Superior has an average depth of nearly 500 feet.
5. The Great Lakes-St. Lawrence River ecosystem includes eight U.S. states and two Canadian provinces.
6. The National Sea Grant Program provides $56 million dollars in competitive research money to fund research in coastal areas, including states bordering the Atlantic and Pacific Oceans, the Gulf of Mexico, and the Great Lakes.
7. Vermont is a landlocked state.
8. The explorer Champlain referred to Lake Ontario as Lake St. Louis in 1632.
9. Lake Champlain borders Vermont, New York, and Canada.

Record your solution and explain it briefly here:

_____

_____

_____

_____

CHAPTER 4, Lesson 7

Visual 7   The Mystery of the Voters Who Don't Vote

Americans are known around the world for their love of liberty and democracy. Many Americans have fought and died to protect their system of government and way of life. Free elections are central to that system of government. Together with safeguards for protecting individual rights, free elections are the heart of American democracy.

Yet many Americans do not vote. Only about half of all eligible voters vote in presidential elections, for example.

Why don't more Americans vote?

Handy Dandy Guide
1. People *choose*.
2. People's choices involve *costs*.
3. People respond to *incentives* in predictable ways.
4. People create *economic systems* that influence individual choices and incentives.
5. People gain when they *trade* voluntarily.
6. People's choices have consequences that lie in the *future*.

CHAPTER 4, Lesson 7

Activity 7   The Mystery of the Voters Who Don't Vote

Directions. Read the *Handy Dandy Guide* and the mystery. Read the clues assigned to your group. Be careful. While all the clues are correct, only some are *useful* in solving the mystery. Decide which clues are most relevant to solving the mystery. Use the clues and one or more of the ideas from the *Handy Dandy Guide* to figure out a solution to the mystery. Write your solution.

Handy Dandy Guide
1. People *choose*.
2. People's choices involve *costs*.
3. People respond to *incentives* in predictable ways.
4. People create *economic systems* that influence individual choices and incentives.
5. People gain when they *trade* voluntarily.
6. People's choices have consequences that lie in the *future*.

The Mystery
Americans are known around the world for their love of liberty and democracy. Many Americans have fought and died to protect their system of government and way of life. Free elections are central to that system of government. Together with safeguards for protecting individual rights, free elections are the heart of American democracy.

Yet many Americans do not vote. Only about half of all eligible voters vote in presidential elections, for example.

Why don't more Americans vote?

The Clues
1. Because of "Motor Voter" legislation and other innovations, it is relatively easy for most Americans to register to vote.
2. At the federal, state, and local levels, there are many elections in the United States. An American who voted in all the elections for which he or she was eligible would do a lot of voting.
3. In presidential elections, long lines of voters often form at the polls.
4. It can be difficult for voters to find reliable information about candidates and issues—especially local candidates and state or local issues addressed in referenda.
5. Each state elects two United States Senators.
6. Few elections in the United States are ever decided by one or two votes.
7. There are two kinds of elections—primary and general.
8. The 26th Amendment to the Constitution made 18 the legal voting age.
9. Voting takes place in polling places.

Record your solution and explain it briefly here:

_____

_____

_____

_____

CHAPTER 4, Lesson 8

Visual 8   The Corny Fuel Mystery

In the midst of the energy crisis late in the 1970s, the U.S. federal government hit on a new idea. Researchers had found ways to mix ethanol—a fuel distilled from corn—with gasoline. This discovery raised hopes that the new fuel mixture might reduce the amount of gasoline Americans used, thus decreasing United States demand for foreign oil while improving air quality.

To encourage the use of ethanol, the federal government provided a subsidy to fuel producers by reducing the gasoline tax on fuel made with the ethanol mixture.

A study done in 1997 by the General Accounting Office of the federal government showed that the ethanol subsidy was expensive (it had cost taxpayers $7 billion since 1979) and did little to improve the environment or reduce imports of foreign oil. However, efforts to abandon the ethanol subsidy have failed to gain approval in Congress.

Why would the United States government provide subsidies for the production of an alternative fuel that does not help the environment, does not reduce consumption of foreign oil, and costs taxpayers billions of dollars?

Handy Dandy Guide
1. People *choose*.
2. People's choices involve *costs*.
3. People respond to *incentives* in predictable ways.
4. People create *economic systems* that influence individual choices and incentives.
5. People gain when they *trade* voluntarily.
6. People's choices have consequences that lie in the *future*.

CHAPTER 4, Lesson 8

Activity 8   The Corny Fuel Mystery

Directions. Read the *Handy Dandy Guide* and the mystery. Read the clues assigned to your group. Be careful. While all the clues are correct, only some are *useful* in solving the mystery. Decide which clues are most relevant to solving the mystery. Use the clues and one or more of the ideas from the *Handy Dandy Guide* to figure out a solution to the mystery. Write your solution.

Handy Dandy Guide
1. People *choose*.
2. People's choices involve *costs*.
3. People respond to *incentives* in predictable ways.
4. People create *economic systems* that influence individual choices and incentives.
5. People gain when they *trade* voluntarily.
6. People's choices have consequences that lie in the *future*.

The Mystery

In the midst of the energy crisis of the late 1970s, the U.S. federal government hit on a new idea. Researchers had found ways to mix ethanol—a fuel distilled from corn—with gasoline. This discovery raised hopes that this new fuel mixture would reduce the amount of gasoline Americans used, thus decreasing United States demand for foreign oil while improving air quality. To encourage the use of ethanol, the federal government provided a subsidy to fuel producers by reducing the gasoline tax on fuel made with the ethanol mixture.

A study done in 1997 by the General Accounting Office (GOA) of the federal government showed that the ethanol subsidy was expensive (it had cost taxpayers $7 billion since 1979) and did little to improve the environment or reduce imports of foreign oil. However, efforts to abandon the ethanol subsidy have failed to gain approval in Congress.

Why would the United States government provide subsidies for the production of an alternative fuel that does not help the environment, does not reduce consumption of foreign oil, and costs taxpayers billions of dollars?

The Clues
1. Environmentalists no longer support ethanol.
2. Many farmers in the Midwest grow corn. Politicians from the Midwest seek votes among the farm population.
3. Farmers in Iowa produce a great deal of corn. Iowa is an important state in national politics because of its early precinct caucus system for selecting delegates to national nominating conventions.
4. Ethanol production adds an estimated $60 million to the economy of South Dakota each year.
5. By 1996, 40 ethanol plants were operating in 20 states, generating 40,000 jobs.
6. The American Corn Growers Alliance supports continued subsidies of ethanol.
7. The real price of oil has been declining in the 1990s.
8. In 1998, Ford Motor Company reported that it had begun experimenting with vehicles designed to use ethanol fuel.
9. Ethanol is sold in more than 40 states.

Record your solution and explain it briefly here:

_____

_____

_____

_____

CHAPTER 4, Lesson 9

Visual 9   The Urban Housing Mystery

While most American cities provide an adequate range of housing possibilities for their citizens, some do not. In New York City, people looking for a place to live typically have a hard time finding apartments. Some of the apartments they find are ones you wouldn't want—units without sinks or hot water, for example. The problem is not a lack of space. New York City has block after block of abandoned apartment buildings.

At the same time, some New Yorkers live in luxury apartments and pay low rents. For example, a 1993 news report stated that former New York City Mayor Ed Koch paid $441 per month in rent for an apartment worth about $1,200 per month at market rental rates.

Why do some New Yorkers face a housing crisis while others are secure in choice apartments, paying low monthly rent?

Handy Dandy Guide
1. People *choose*.
2. People's choices involve *costs*.
3. People respond to *incentives* in predictable ways.
4. People create *economic systems* that influence individual choices and incentives.
5. People gain when they *trade* voluntarily.
6. People's choices have consequences that lie in the *future*.

CHAPTER 4, Lesson 9

Activity 9 The Urban Housing Mystery

Directions. Read the *Handy Dandy Guide* and the mystery. Read the clues assigned to your group. Be careful. While all the clues are correct, only some are *useful* in solving the mystery. Decide which clues are most relevant to solving the mystery. Use the clues and one or more of the ideas from the *Handy Dandy Guide* to figure out a solution to the mystery. Write your solution.

Handy Dandy Guide
1. People *choose*.
2. People's choices involve *costs*.
3. People respond to *incentives* in predictable ways.
4. People create *economic systems* that influence individual choices and incentives.
5. People gain when they *trade* voluntarily.
6. People's choices have consequences that lie in the *future*.

The Mystery
While most American cities provide an adequate range of housing possibilities for their citizens, some do not. In New York City, people looking for a place to live typically have a hard time finding apartments. Some of the apartments they find are ones you wouldn't want—units without sinks or hot water, for example. The problem is not a lack of space. New York City has block after block of abandoned apartment buildings.

At the same time, some New Yorkers live in luxury apartments and pay low rents. For example, a 1993 news report stated that former New York City Mayor Ed Koch paid $441 per month for an apartment worth about $1,200 per month at market rental rates.

Why do some New Yorkers face a housing crisis while others are secure in choice apartments, paying low monthly rent?

The Clues
1. During World War II, New York City began using a system of rent controls that set the rent of many apartments below the market price.
2. Rents are incentives to landlords, affecting the decisions they make about providing rental units.
3. The population of metropolitan New York is 17,953,372.
4. The total area of all five New York City boroughs (Manhattan, Brooklyn, Bronx, Queens and Staten Island) is 301 square miles.
5. New York is not the most dangerous of the large U.S. cities.
6. In most cities, when rental rates for apartments go up, builders begin to build new apartment units.
7. In New York City, many wealthy people—including former mayors and wealthy actors—live in apartments where they pay far below market prices for rent.
8. Some people who live in rent-controlled apartments are able to hand the apartments down to their family members. They never give them up.
9. Yankee Stadium is called The House that Ruth Built.

Record your solution and explain it briefly here:

_____

_____

_____

CHAPTER 4, Lesson 10

Visual 10   The Mystery of the Unwanted Melons

In the early 1990s, some U.S. farmers who ordinarily grew cotton and peanuts began planting crops that were unusual for them—squash and melons, for example.

Many of these farmers did not take good care of their new crops. They planted them at odd times, did not irrigate them, and generally did not attend to them. In fact, they hoped they would never harvest these new crops.

Why would farmers plant crops they do not want to harvest?

Handy Dandy Guide
1. People *choose*.
2. People's choices involve *costs*.
3. People respond to *incentives* in predictable ways.
4. People create *economic systems* that influence individual choices and incentives.
5. People gain when they *trade* voluntarily.
6. People's choices have consequences that lie in the *future*.

CHAPTER 4, Lesson 10

Activity 10   The Mystery of the Unwanted Melons

Directions. Read the *Handy Dandy Guide* and the mystery. Read the clues assigned to your group. Be careful. While all the clues are correct, only some are *useful* in solving the mystery. Decide which clues are most relevant to solving the mystery. Use the clues and one or more of the ideas from the *Handy Dandy Guide* to figure out a solution to the mystery. Write your solution.

Handy Dandy Guide
1. People *choose*.
2. People's choices involve *costs*.
3. People respond to *incentives* in predictable ways.
4. People create *economic systems* that influence individual choices and incentives.
5. People gain when they *trade* voluntarily.
6. People's choices have consequences that lie in the *future*.

The Mystery
In the early 1990s, some U.S. farmers who ordinarily grew cotton and peanuts began planting crops that were unusual for them—squash and melons, for example. Many of these farmers did not take good care of their new crops. They planted them at odd times, did not irrigate them, and generally did not attend to them. In fact, they hoped they would never harvest these new crops.

Why would farmers plant crops they do not want to harvest?

The Clues
1. Millions of dollars are paid each year to compensate farmers for crops that fail.
2. The number of crops eligible for crop-failure payments has grown and now includes 14 types of melons, 22 kinds of beans, and 86 flowers.
3. Congress declares crop disasters about once a year.
4. The number of farms in the United States peaked at 6.8 million in 1935.
5. Today, there are fewer than two million farms in the United States.
6. In 1993, American farmers received $22 billion in farm subsidies (payments from the government).
7. Success in farming depends a great deal on weather conditions.
8. In New Zealand, only 4 percent of farm income derives from subsidies.
9. One U.S. government audit identified $92.5 million in questionable payments to farmers requesting compensation for crop failures.

Record your solution and explain it briefly here:

_____

_____

_____

_____

CHAPTER 4, Lesson 11

Visual 11   Why Can't You Buy a Car On Sunday?

Shopping during weekdays is difficult for today's double-income families. Yet the law in 21 states requires car dealerships to remain closed on Sundays.

This might seem odd. Business people generally claim that they do not want government to interfere with their business practices. But when one Minnesota legislator proposed that car sales be permitted (not required) on Sundays, he drew strong opposition from the Minnesota Auto Dealers Association.

Why would people who sell cars not want to sell them on Sunday?

Handy Dandy Guide
1. People *choose*.
2. People's choices involve *costs*.
3. People respond to *incentives* in predictable ways.
4. People create *economic systems* that influence individual choices and incentives.
5. People gain when they *trade* voluntarily.
6. People's choices have consequences that lie in the *future*.

CHAPTER 4, Lesson 11

Activity 11 Why Can't You Buy A car on Sunday?

Directions. Read the *Handy Dandy Guide* and the mystery. Read the clues assigned to your group. Be careful. While all the clues are correct, only some are *useful* in solving the mystery. Decide which clues are most relevant to solving the mystery. Use the clues and one or more of the ideas from the *Handy Dandy Guide* to figure out a solution to the mystery. Write your solution.

Handy Dandy Guide
1. People *choose*.
2. People's choices involve *costs*.
3. People respond to *incentives* in predictable ways.
4. People create *economic systems* that influence individual choices and incentives.
5. People gain when they *trade* voluntarily.
6. People's choices have consequences that lie in the *future*.

The Mystery
Shopping during weekdays is difficult for today's double-income families. Yet the law in 21 states requires car dealerships to remain closed on Sundays. This may seem odd. Most often business leaders claim they do not want government to interfere with their business practices. Yet when one Minnesota legislator proposed that car sales be permitted (not required) on Sundays, he drew strong opposition from the Minnesota Auto Dealers Association.

Why would people who sell cars not want to sell them on Sunday?

The Clues
1. The percentage of Americans claiming an affiliation with organized religion has decreased steadily in the last half of the 20th century.
2. Most "blue laws" (laws prohibiting commerce on Sundays) have been abolished.
3. Acquiring accurate information about a car purchase or lease takes time.
4. The "sticker price" of a car on a sales floor may or may not be the actual price of the car.
5. Comparison shopping for a car takes time.
6. Many people who earn their living selling cars prefer to be home with their families on Sundays.
7. Minnesota passed its law requiring car dealers to be closed on Sundays in 1957.
8. People who earn their living selling cars have a reputation for being aggressive.
9. Limiting showroom hours has been challenged in some states as an illegal effort to reduce competition.

Record your solution and explain it briefly here:

_____

_____

_____

_____

CHAPTER 5

Environmental Mysteries

Chapter 5 presents the Visuals and Activity sheets you will need for lessons 1-8.

Each Visual includes one mystery, along with the *Handy Dandy Guide*. Each Activity sheet recaps the mystery and the *HDG*, for students' easy reference; each Activity sheet also presents clues and provides space in which students should write out their solutions.

The objective of environmental policy is to achieve a cleaner environment. And, since our resources are scarce, we do not want to waste them (that is, to use more of them than necessary) in pursuing our goal of environmental protection. The contribution of economics is to show how markets and private property rights can create strong incentives for improving environmental quality while reducing the cost of achieving it.

A key contribution of an economics approach to the environment is helping people recognize the notion of the "tragedy of the commons." Biologist Garrett Hardin described the "tragedy of the commons" in a seminal 1968 article in *Science*.

Hardin describes a commonly-owned pasture. In such a pasture, the individual who adds a cow (when the pasture is full) receives the full benefit of the additional cow, but does not pay the full cost of using up the pasture. That cost is shared among all the villagers who own livestock. The result, as long as access is open to all, will be overgrazing and ultimately destruction of the commons. In a commons with open access, each person has an incentive to take action that is costly for the group as a whole because the cost is shared, while the benefits are individually enjoyed.

Public parks are often cited as examples of the commons. Park visitors have little incentive to keep them clean—anyone, at anytime, can mess them up again—and there is no owner who benefits financially by making sure the park is well kept. Air and water are often polluted because they, too, are a commons. They have no owners to keep people from using them for waste, so polluters gain the benefits of getting rid of their waste while sharing the cost with many others.

Another example relates to wildlife. The bison came close to extinction because they were commonly owned. Hunters obtained the benefits of killing what they could, while the cost—the gradual decline in numbers to near-extinction—was shared among everyone. Hunters wanted bison, and because they were commonly owned no one had an incentive to protect a herd for the future. Today, much wildlife is endangered because it is a commons.

The fact that markets for clean air, water, and bison are hard to set up is a significant cause of environmental harm. Conversely, finding ways to establish the features of markets in regard to the environment—for example, experiments with establishing ownership rights in fisheries—can be an effective tool for improving the environment.

CHAPTER 5, Lesson 1

Visual 1 Why Haven't We Run Out of Natural Resources

The earth today supports about 6 billion people. Most of these people live in a condition of poverty, lacking adequate food, water, housing, and medical care. As this population grows and its needs continue to increase, many people fear that increasing demand for the earth's resources will deplete those resources drastically. Some scientists in the 1970s predicted, for example, that the world would run out of oil and many important minerals by the 1990s.

After the close of the 1990s, however, things look different. There is little talk today about exhausting our mineral supplies. Prices for most commodities are stable, suggesting a stable supply. Oil reserves have actually increased. People in impoverished places continue to face shortages, but those shortages have nothing to do with shortages of natural resources. Every recent famine, for example, has been caused by civil wars, ethnic disputes, or natural catastrophes—not the exhaustion of natural resources.

How can this be? If our natural resources are finite and the world's population is growing, why haven't we run out of resources?

Handy Dandy Guide
1. People *choose*.
2. People's choices involve *costs*.
3. People respond to *incentives* in predictable ways.
4. People create *economic systems* that influence individual choices and incentives.
5. People gain when they *trade* voluntarily.
6. People's choices have consequences that lie in the *future*.

CHAPTER 5, Lesson 1

Activity 1   Why Haven't We Run Out of Resources?

Directions. Read the *Handy Dandy Guide* and the mystery. Read the clues assigned to your group. Be careful. While all the clues are correct, only some are *useful* in solving the mystery. Decide which clues are most relevant to solving the mystery. Use the clues and one or more of the ideas from the *Handy Dandy Guide* to figure out a solution to the mystery. Write your solution.

Handy Dandy Guide
1. People *choose*.
2. People's choices involve *costs*.
3. People respond to *incentives* in predictable ways.
4. People create *economic systems* that influence individual choices and incentives.
5. People gain when they *trade* voluntarily.
6. People's choices have consequences that lie in the *future*.

The Mystery
The earth today supports about 6 billion people. Most of these people live in a condition of poverty, lacking adequate food, water, housing, and medical care. As this population grows and its needs increase, many people fear that increasing demand for the earth's resources will deplete those resources drastically. Some scientists in the 1970s predicted, for example, that the world would run out of oil and many important minerals by the 1990s.

After the close of the 1990s, however, things look different. There is little talk today about exhausting our mineral supplies. Prices for most commodities have been stable, suggesting a stable supply. Oil reserves have actually increased. People in impoverished places continue to face shortages, but those shortages have nothing to do with natural resources. Every recent famine, for example, has been caused by civil war, ethnic disputes, or natural catastrophes—not the exhaustion of natural resources.

How can this be? If our natural resources are finite and the world's population is growing, why haven't we run out of natural resources?

The Clues
1. In 1978, proven oil reserves stood at 648 billion barrels—enough to last 29.9 years at 1978 rates of consumption. By 1992, proven oil reserves had increased to 999 billion barrels of oil.
2. The U.S. Department of Energy uses a variety of programs to conserve natural resources.
3. There is a scarcity of dollars to do scientific research on resource conservation.
4. If the price of a natural resource begins to increase, consumers increase efforts at conservation.
5. If the price of a natural resource begins to increase, producers increase efforts to find more of the resource.
6. Some people predict that the earth's population will increase to 10 billion.
7. Thomas Malthus was among the first to predict that population growth would soon outstrip the earth's ability to feed its people.
8. Oil companies face competition and, as a result, are searching for ways to lower the costs of oil production. This allows producers the chance to earn higher profits while lowering prices for consumers.

Record your solution and explain it briefly here:

_____
_____
_____
_____

CHAPTER 5, Lesson 2

Visual 2 Why Air Condition the Desert?

Water is a scarce resource. It is precious, especially in arid places and in areas where many people live.

Yet in upscale shopping centers and resort areas in the southwestern United States, people try to cool the hot summer temperatures by using misters that emit a light spray of water into the air above sidewalks and patios, thus taking the edge off the desert heat.

Why would people in the middle of the desert use their scarce water resources to "air condition" the outdoors?

Handy Dandy Guide
1. People *choose*.
2. People's choices involve *costs*.
3. People respond to *incentives* in predictable ways.
4. People create *economic systems* that influence individual choices and incentives.
5. People gain when they *trade* voluntarily.
6. People's choices have consequences that lie in the *future*.

CHAPTER 5, Lesson 2

Activity 2   Why Air Condition the Desert?

Directions. Read the *Handy Dandy Guide* and the mystery. Read the clues assigned to your group. Be careful. While all the clues are correct, only some are *useful* in solving the mystery. Decide which clues are most relevant to solving the mystery. Use the clues and one or more of the ideas from the *Handy Dandy Guide* to figure out a solution to the mystery. Write your solution.

Handy Dandy Guide
1. People *choose*.
2. People's choices involve *costs*.
3. People respond to *incentives* in predictable ways.
4. People create *economic systems* that influence individual choices and incentives.
5. People gain when they *trade* voluntarily.
6. People's choices have consequences that lie in the *future*.

The Mystery
Water is a scarce resource. It is precious, especially in arid places and in areas where many people live. Yet in upscale shopping centers and resort areas in the southwestern United States, people try to cool the hot summer temperatures by using misters to emit a light spray of water into the air above sidewalks and patios, thus taking the edge off the desert heat.

Why would people in the middle of the desert use their scarce water resources to "air condition" the outdoors?

The Clues
1. Government-sponsored irrigation projects provide water at low prices in the southwestern United States.
2. The Environmental Protection Agency conducts water audits free of charge to encourage people to stretch water supplies by repairing leaky faucets and using low-flow plumbing.
3. Concerned about damage to the environment, the Environmental Protection Agency suggests that dam construction should be avoided wherever possible.
4. The West is the fastest growing region of the United States.
5. The West is the most arid region of the United States.
6. The average high temperature in Phoenix during June and July is about 105 degrees.
7. Most of the water produced by federal water projects is used for irrigating crops.

Record your solution and explain it briefly here:

_____

_____

_____

_____

CHAPTER 5, Lesson 3

Visual 3 Why Grow Rice in the Desert?

We think of farmers as sensible, practical people, inclined to make prudent decisions about their work.

But sometimes farmers make decisions that seem very strange. For example, farmers in California grow large crops of rice (which requires a great deal of water) in the desert (the Sacramento Valley).

Why would farmers grow rice in the desert?

Handy Dandy Guide
1. People *choose*.
2. People's choices involve *costs*.
3. People respond to *incentives* in predictable ways.
4. People create *economic systems* that influence individual choices and incentives.
5. People gain when they *trade* voluntarily.
6. People's choices have consequences that lie in the *future*.

CHAPTER 5, Lesson 3

Activity 3   Why Grow Rice in the Desert?

Directions. Read the *Handy Dandy Guide* and the mystery. Read the clues assigned to your group. Be careful. While all the clues are correct, only some are *useful* in solving the mystery. Decide which clues are most relevant to solving the mystery. Use the clues and one or more of the ideas from the *Handy Dandy Guide* to figure out a solution to the mystery. Write your solution.

Handy Dandy Guide
1. People *choose*.
2. People's choices involve *costs*.
3. People respond to *incentives* in predictable ways.
4. People create *economic systems* that influence individual choices and incentives.
5. People gain when they *trade* voluntarily.
6. People's choices have consequences that lie in the *future*.

The Mystery
We think of farmers as sensible, practical people, inclined to make prudent decisions about their work. But farmers sometimes make decisions that seem very strange. For example, farmers in California grow large crops of rice (which requires a great deal of water) in the desert (the Sacramento Valley).

Why would farmers grow rice in the desert?

The Clues
1. Farmers in California are able to earn an income growing and selling rice.
2. Most of the water used in growing rice comes from government-sponsored irrigation projects.
3. The price California farmers pay for water used in irrigation is well below the market price. The farmers get a substantial discount.
4. Starting in 1902, the federal government began to subsidize construction of large water storage and delivery projects.
5. In periods of severe drought, Californians are warned against flushing toilets, watering lawns, and taking showers.
6. Rice is grown in many parts of the world, especially in Asia.
7. California farmers, like farmers everywhere, have good years (sunshine and adequate rain) and bad years (drought).
8. Many grape producers in California went out of business in the 1980s.

Record your solution and explain it briefly here:

_____

_____

_____

_____

===== CHAPTER 5, Lesson 4 =====

Visual 4   The Tragedy of the Commons

Wildlife is in danger in many parts of the world.

- Fishing fleets catch so many wild salmon that the species is threatened.

- In some parts of Africa, elephants and other animals are hunted by poachers, despite government bans on hunting.

- The world's population of whales is in danger.

Why are so many wild animals endangered?

Handy Dandy Guide
1. People *choose*.
2. People's choices involve *costs*.
3. People respond to *incentives* in predictable ways.
4. People create *economic systems* that influence individual choices and incentives.
5. People gain when they *trade* voluntarily.
6. People's choices have consequences that lie in the *future*.

CHAPTER 5, Lesson 4

Activity 4 The Tragedy of the Commons

Directions. Read the *Handy Dandy Guide* and the mystery. Read the clues assigned to your group. Be careful. While all the clues are correct, only some are *useful* in solving the mystery. Decide which clues are most relevant to solving the mystery. Use the clues and one or more of the ideas from the *Handy Dandy Guide* to figure out a solution to the mystery. Write your solution.

Handy Dandy Guide
1. People *choose*.
2. People's choices involve *costs*.
3. People respond to *incentives* in predictable ways.
4. People create *economic systems* that influence individual choices and incentives.
5. People gain when they *trade* voluntarily.
6. People's choices have consequences that lie in the *future*.

The Mystery
Wildlife is in danger in many parts of the world.

- Fishing fleets catch so many wild salmon that the species is threatened.
- In some parts of Africa, elephants and other animals are hunted by poachers, despite government bans on hunting.
- The world's population of whales is in danger.

Why are so many wild animals endangered?

The Clues
1. Each problem involves an environmental issue.
2. Each problem has frustrated efforts by governments to come up with practical and effective solutions.
3. Each problem involves a lack of incentives for conservation.
4. Each problem involves something not owned by individuals—fish and wildlife.
5. Each problem is very old—the subject of long struggles.
6. Each problem is often used as an example of how people are bad, so that their behavior must be curbed through regulation.

Record your solution and explain it briefly here:

_____

_____

_____

_____

CHAPTER 5, Lesson 5

Visual 5 The Dark Side of Curbside Recycling

Many Americans are taught at an early age about the importance of recycling. Most of us dutifully separate paper, plastic, glass, and cans and haul these things down to the curb on the assigned day of the week. We all feel better knowing we are helping our community and the environment.

Yet some critics have argued that curbside recycling may actually harm our community and the environment.

How could there be a downside to something as benign as recycling? How can recycling harm our environment?

Handy Dandy Guide
1. People *choose*.
2. People's choices involve *costs*.
3. People respond to *incentives* in predictable ways.
4. People create *economic systems* that influence individual choices and incentives.
5. People gain when they *trade* voluntarily.
6. People's choices have consequences that lie in the *future*.

CHAPTER 5, Lesson 5

Activity 5   The Dark Side of Curbside Recycling

Directions. Read the *Handy Dandy Guide* and the mystery. Read the clues assigned to your group. Be careful. While all the clues are correct, only some are *useful* in solving the mystery. Decide which clues are most relevant to solving the mystery. Use the clues and one or more of the ideas from the *Handy Dandy Guide* to figure out a solution to the mystery. Write your solution.

Handy Dandy Guide
1. People *choose*.
2. People's choices involve *costs*.
3. People respond to *incentives* in predictable ways.
4. People create *economic systems* that influence individual choices and incentives.
5. People gain when they *trade* voluntarily.
6. People's choices have consequences that lie in the *future*.

The Mystery
Many Americans are taught at an early age about the importance of recycling. Most of us dutifully separate paper, plastic, glass, and cans and haul these things down to the curb on the assigned day of the week. We all feel better knowing we are helping our community and the environment.

Yet some critics have argued that curbside recycling may actually harm our community and the environment.

How could there be a downside to something as benign as recycling? How can recycling harm our environment?

The Clues
1. Recycling is not a new idea. Aluminum, glass, copper, and iron are among the materials people have recycled for many years. They have recycled these materials because they have market value; somebody is willing to buy them.
2. Much of the waste collected at the curb for recycling has no market value.
3. Community groups once used "paper sales" as a way to raise money. Sales projects of this sort have been made obsolete by curbside recycling programs.
4. Since it is common to have two haulers of curbside waste—one for the garbage and one for material to be recycled—the amount of energy used to collect waste, and the pollution emitted by trucks used in collections, is now twice the amount it would otherwise be.
5. Many cities have special programs to educate the public about the importance of recycling.
6. The vast majority of Americans cooperate with local government's recycling plans.
7. Landfill space is available in most cities. Some cities compete to get the garbage of others.
8. The per capita production of solid waste by American households has remained steady through 2000.

Record your solution and explain it briefly here:

_____

_____

_____

_____

CHAPTER 5, Lesson 6

Visual 6   The Bright Side of Urban Sprawl

Americans continue to be mobile people, relocating themselves to outlying areas beyond the established suburbs.

Yet it is fashionable in some circles to hate urban sprawl. The term itself—"urban sprawl"—sounds bad. To many Americans it conjures up images of endless strip malls and congested roadways crowding out a dwindling supply of open spaces. Some politicians have argued for an end to unregulated urban sprawl, proposing instead that growth should conform to "smart growth" plans.

If urban sprawl is such a bad thing, why do so many Americans choose to be a part of it?

Handy Dandy Guide
1. People *choose*.
2. People's choices involve *costs*.
3. People respond to *incentives* in predictable ways.
4. People create *economic systems* that influence individual choices and incentives.
5. People gain when they *trade* voluntarily.
6. People's choices have consequences that lie in the *future*.

CHAPTER 5, Lesson 6

Activity 6   The Bright Side of Urban Sprawl

Directions. Read the *Handy Dandy Guide* and the mystery. Read the clues assigned to your group. Be careful. While all the clues are correct, only some are *useful* in solving the mystery. Decide which clues are most relevant to solving the mystery. Use the clues and one or more of the ideas from the *Handy Dandy Guide* to figure out a solution to the mystery. Write your solution.

Handy Dandy Guide
1. People *choose*.
2. People's choices involve *costs*.
3. People respond to *incentives* in predictable ways.
4. People create *economic systems* that influence individual choices and incentives.
5. People gain when they *trade* voluntarily.
6. People's choices have consequences that lie in the *future*.

The Mystery
Americans continue to be mobile people, relocating themselves to outlying areas beyond the established suburbs. Yet it is fashionable in some circles to hate urban sprawl. The very term—"urban sprawl"— sounds bad. To many Americans it conjures up images of endless strip malls and congested roadways, crowding out a dwindling supply of open spaces. Some politicians have argued for an end to unregulated urban sprawl, proposing instead that growth should conform to plans for "smart growth."

If urban sprawl is such a bad thing, why do so many Americans choose to be a part of it?

The Clues
1. Some urban sprawl involves people "leap frogging" over open areas to developments outside the established suburbs. People are attracted to "leap frog" developments because they increase the supply of affordable housing.
2. Over 95 percent of the land in the United States is not developed.
3. Many people enjoy living in less congested areas. Three quarters of retired farmland is retained as open space, in the form of forests, parks, pastures, and rural wildlife preserves.
4. Many urban sprawlers face longer commutes to jobs on over-crowded roads.
5. Urban sprawl often proceeds faster than local services—such as water, sewers, schools, and roads— can be developed.
6. Some strip mall or "big box" commercial developments are considered ugly by government planners and residents.
7. Most people live and work in the same community—rural, urban, or suburban.
8. Low density housing developments (big homes built on large lots) use land but do little environmental damage. In fact, the open space and environmental quality are part of the attraction for newcomers.

Record your solution and explain it briefly here:

_____

_____

_____

_____

CHAPTER 5, Lesson 7

Visual 7 How Can Trading Emissions Rights Reduce Pollution?

In 1995, the Environmental Protection Agency reported that levels of six major air pollutants had decreased by 29 percent over the preceding 25 years. Much of the improvement could be attributed to government regulations, such as rules requiring the removal of lead from gasoline.

But that is not the whole story. Much recent improvement in air quality has been attained by means of an environmental program that relies on market forces. The government provides factories in a city with a specific number of pollution permits. A company then may discharge emissions up to the limit set in its permits, or it may sell some of its emissions allotment to other companies.

This plan actually allows some people to pollute more than others. How could selling pollution rights reduce pollution?

Handy Dandy Guide
1. People *choose*.
2. People's choices involve *costs*.
3. People respond to *incentives* in predictable ways.
4. People create *economic systems* that influence individual choices and incentives.
5. People gain when they *trade* voluntarily.
6. People's choices have consequences that lie in the *future*.

CHAPTER 5, Lesson 7

Activity 7   How Can Trading Emissions Rights Reduce Pollution?

Directions. Read the *Handy Dandy Guide* and the mystery. Read the clues assigned to your group. Be careful. While all the clues are correct, only some are *useful* in solving the mystery. Decide which clues are most relevant to solving the mystery. Use the clues and one or more of the ideas from the *Handy Dandy Guide* to figure out a solution to the mystery. Write your solution.

Handy Dandy Guide
1. People *choose*.
2. People's choices involve *costs*.
3. People respond to *incentives* in predictable ways.
4. People create *economic systems* that influence individual choices and incentives.
5. People gain when they *trade* voluntarily.
6. People's choices have consequences that lie in the *future*.

The Mystery
In 1995, the Environmental Protection Agency reported that levels of six major air pollutants had decreased by 29 percent over the preceding 25 years. Much of the improvement could be attributed to government regulations, such as rules requiring the removal of lead from gasoline.

But that is not the whole story. Much recent improvement in air quality has been attained by means of an environmental program that relies on market forces. The government provides factories in a city with a specific number of pollution permits. A company then may discharge emissions up to the limit set in its permits, or it may sell some of its emissions allotment to other companies.

This plan actually allows some people to pollute more that others. How could selling emissions rights reduce pollution?

The Clues
1. Some businesses (those with modern plants, for example) can reduce their pollutant emissions more efficiently than other businesses.
2. Despite a growing economy, emissions of man-made carbon dioxide remained almost flat in the United States from 1997 to 1998.
3. Emissions trading begins with a government-set target for the reduction of overall emissions in a given location.
4. Emissions trading in the United States has been such a success that many government leaders now favor development of a plan for international trading of pollution rights.
5. Burning oil, gas, and other fossil fuels releases carbon dioxide into the atmosphere.
6. Carbon dioxide is the main "greenhouse" gas that some scientists think is overheating the planet by trapping the sun's rays in the atmosphere.
7. In the United States, emissions of lead into the air declined by 98 percent from 1970 to 1994.
8. Purchasing emission rights is a cost. Over time, businesses strive to reduce their costs.

Record your solution and explain it briefly here:

_____

_____

_____

_____

======= CHAPTER 5, Lesson 8 =======

Visual 8 Why Are Our National Parks Crumbling?

We love our National Parks. In fact, we may be loving them to death. U.S. National Park managers report all kinds of serious problems.

- Campgrounds are closed.
- Roads are crumbling.
- Buildings are in disrepair.
- Maintenance is years behind.

Yet many state parks, including those in Texas, South Dakota, and Arkansas, are offering new services to park users and are increasing their revenues.

Why are national parks crumbling while state parks are thriving?

Handy Dandy Guide
1. People *choose*.
2. People's choices involve *costs*.
3. People respond to *incentives* in predictable ways.
4. People create *economic systems* that influence individual choices and incentives.
5. People gain when they *trade* voluntarily.
6. People's choices have consequences that lie in the *future*.

CHAPTER 5, Lesson 8

Activity 8   Why Are Our National Parks Crumbling?

Directions. Read the *Handy Dandy Guide* and the mystery. Read the clues assigned to your group. Be careful. While all the clues are correct, only some are *useful* in solving the mystery. Decide which clues are most relevant to solving the mystery. Use the clues and one or more of the ideas from the *Handy Dandy Guide* to figure out a solution to the mystery. Write your solution.

Handy Dandy Guide
1. People *choose*.
2. People's choices involve *costs*.
3. People respond to *incentives* in predictable ways.
4. People create *economic systems* that influence individual choices and incentives.
5. People gain when they *trade* voluntarily.
6. People's choices have consequences that lie in the *future*.

The Mystery
We love our National Parks. In fact, we may be loving them to death. U.S. National Park managers report all kinds of serious problems.

- Campgrounds are closed.
- Roads are crumbling.
- Buildings are in disrepair.
- Maintenance is years behind.

Yet many state parks, including those in Texas, South Dakota, and Arkansas, are offering new services to park users and are increasing their revenues.

Why are national parks crumbling while state parks are thriving?

The Clues
1. On August 25, 1916, President Woodrow Wilson signed an act creating the National Park Service.
2. The National Park System of the United States occupies more than 83 million acres.
3. In 1872, Congress established Yellowstone National Park in the Territories of Montana and Wyoming "as a public park or pleasuring ground for the benefit and enjoyment of the people."
4. In 1918, a federal law was passed requiring that all revenues from the National Parks be turned over to the U.S. general treasury.
5. The founding of Yellowstone National Park began a worldwide national park movement. Today more than 100 nations contain some 1,200 national parks or equivalent preserves.
6. Many state parks in Texas and South Dakota rely on user fees—not general revenues from the state legislature—to operate the parks. Parks are encouraged to be self-reliant.
7. The National Park Service reported a $500 million maintenance backlog in 1998.
8. In 1915, Stephen Mather was appointed the first director of the National Park Service.

Record your solution and explain it briefly here:

_____

_____

_____

_____

CHAPTER 6

Writing Your Own Mysteries

We hope you have had fun thinking about the mysteries we've collected for you. Now we hope to interest you in collecting mysteries of your own.

Our book is open-ended. The world is filled with economic mysteries waiting to be noticed and put to use. You can pick up where we left off. Better yet, you can set your students to the task of finding new mysteries. New ones don't come along every day, but once you and your students get your antennae up you can find enough good mysteries in your time together to enrich your courses considerably. Here are a few suggestions for the task.

Be on the Lookout for Things That Seem Odd

Economic mystery writers pay attention to the news. This is where most of our mysteries come from. While many newspapers and news magazines provide a rich source of possibilities, we have found that the *Wall Street Journal* and the *New York Times* are unusually good sources.

But it isn't enough merely to scan the news in search of stories about economics. The key is to look for oddities, anomalies, curiosities—discrepancies between a reported event or state of affairs and your own sense of what ought to be expected under the circumstances. Discrepancies of this sort invite explanatory efforts; they provide, therefore, excellent focal points for exercises in economic reasoning.

For example, we often read headlines about teacher shortages. Teachers know that shortages do exist. In many states, it is nearly impossible to find physics or a technology teacher. The U.S. Department of Education predicts that we will need 2.2 million new teachers over the next decade.

But teachers also know that there are plenty of new teachers—even large surpluses—in some teaching fields. For example, colleges and universities in many states produce surplus numbers of social studies and health teachers. This looks like a mystery. How can we have simultaneous shortages and surpluses of teachers? Can the apparent anomaly be explained by economic reasoning?

Develop a Primary Proposition

Once you have noticed a problem, describe one side of it in a straightforward assertion. We call this a primary proposition. For example:

> In 1995, the National Highway Traffic Safety Administration predicted that the expected repeal of the federally mandated 55 miles per hour speed limit would result in an additional 6,400 highway fatalities each year.

The primary proposition states something that is generally known or something that looks reasonable on the face of it. Certainly, it can be difficult to control cars driven at high speeds. It is not surprising, therefore, that allowing states to push speed limits back up to 65 miles per hour seemed like a dangerous idea.

Develop an Opposing Proposition

If you really are onto a good mystery, the facts of the case will suggest information that runs counter to the primary proposition in some interesting way, undercutting it or at least qualifying it. When you come upon counter-examples or counter-arguments of this sort, state them in an opposing proposition, thus implying a mystery or area of uncertainty that needs explaining.

Staying with the speed limit mystery, here is an opposing proposition:

CHAPTER 6

[But] In 1998 the National Highway Traffic Safety Administration announced that fatalities on U.S. highways had fallen to 41,480-- down from 41,817 in 1995.

The information conveyed by the opposing proposition runs counter to the prediction (often it is a generalization) reported in the primary proposition. In thinking about opposing propositions, you might find it helpful to notice that it is always possible to begin an opposing proposition with "yet" or "but" or "however."

Identify the Mystery Explicitly

By itself, the juxtaposition of the two main propositions is apt to suggest pretty clearly what the mystery is. But it is important nonetheless to identify that mystery explicitly, so that you know for sure what it is that needs explaining.

Again, staying with the highway safety mystery:

What is going on here? What could explain an observed decrease in automobile crash fatalities following an increase in the legal speed limit?

Focus on Economic Principles in Trying to Explain the Mystery

Set aside non-economic ways of looking at the mystery. Don't trivialize it, for example, by invoking prefabricated cautions about possible measurement problems ("Maybe the new highway statistics are inaccurate") or bias ("Maybe the new Director of the Traffic Safety Administration likes to drive fast"). Measurement problems, observer bias, and other non-economic considerations may fit the facts in a given case, of course, but when they are called upon prematurely or routinely they act as thought-stoppers, preventing people from looking into aspects of the problem that may prove to be far more important and interesting.

The principles of the *Handy Dandy Guide* can help you maintain your economic focus. Those principles highlight, for example, the importance of getting the incentives straight in any analysis of an economic mystery. You may have observed that nearly every one of the economic mysteries in this book can be resolved or clarified in large measure by attention to the incentives at stake. Test the point out against the speed limit mystery. How might a change in highway speed limits alter the incentives that influence the drivers' choices?

Taken together, the *Handy Dandy Guide* principles also highlight the importance of looking beyond what seems obvious. It may seem obvious that if speed limits are increased, more people will be killed on our roads and highways. But in an economic system, one change (a change in incentives, for example) ordinarily leads to several others, with results that can be anything but obvious. In economic reasoning, therefore, we need to keep alert for possible secondary effects or unintended consequences.

Here's the example we've been leading up to—the one about speed limits and highway safety. How might economic principles explain the mystery of fewer deaths at higher speed limits? Let's start at the beginning. Drivers make choices about how fast to drive. Drivers try to make choices that will yield the best combination of costs and benefits. What costs? The cost (in dollars and other losses) of getting hurt in an accident, for example, or the cost of paying for a speeding ticket. Another sort of cost has to do with the value of the driver's time. Getting to destinations faster, or on time according to an anticipated schedule, is an important benefit for many drivers, and it creates an incentive to move along. How fast? It depends on how the driver weighs the potential cost of getting hurt, of getting ticketed, and so on.

Pressing this line of thought further, Stephan Moore of the Cato Institute moved on to the question of why deaths decreased when speed limits went up. According to his analysis, one effect of increasing highway speed limits is to reduce travel times on highways. The prospect of reduced travel time presents drivers with a new incentive. It is an incentive to drive on the highways with higher speed limits, since those highways get you where you're going, faster. But stop and think: *The same incentive encourages drivers to abandon the more dangerous secondary roads.* Head-on crashes and other fatal accidents are more common on secondary roads due in large part to two-way traffic on narrow roads. The shift by drivers to more highway driving might increase *highway* fatalities, but if that increase is offset by a larger decrease in fatalities on the secondary roads, the net effect will be fewer fatalities overall. Notice that this hypothesis is testable. One could look to see whether the fatality rates in question did in fact break down in the manner suggested by Moore's analysis.

Pretty neat, we think. Economic reasoning—guided by an accessible set of principles, and attentive to secondary effects—yields a fresh analysis of a problem and invites further investigation. We hope you and your students will enjoy similar outcomes in your work with economic mysteries.

Let Us Know

We're still collecting mysteries. If you or your students find some good ones, we'd be grateful if you'd let us see them. You can reach us at **mschug@uwm.edu.**